DISCOVERING PAQUIMÉ

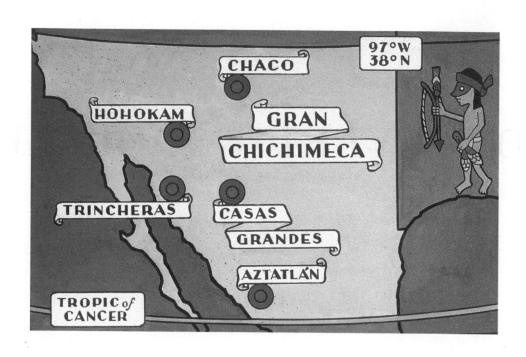

DISCOVERING PAQUIMÉ

EDITED BY

PAUL E. MINNIS AND **MICHAEL E. WHALEN**

THE UNIVERSITY OF
ARIZONA PRESS

AMERIND
FOUNDATION

TUCSON AND DRAGOON

The University of Arizona Press and the Amerind Foundation
www.uapress.arizona.edu
www.amerind.org

Printed in the United States of America
21   20   19   18   17   16   6   5   4   3   2   1

Cover designed by Leigh McDonald
Cover photo courtesy of the Amerind Foundation, Inc., Dragoon, Arizona. Amerind Photographic
Catalog No. CG/A.10F.2.

Support for this publication was provided by the Arizona Archaeological and
Historical Society.

Library of Congress Cataloging-in-Publication Data
Names: Minnis, Paul E., editor. | Whalen, Michael E., editor.
Title: Discovering Paquimé / edited by Paul E. Minnis and Michael E. Whalen.
Description: Tucson : The University of Arizona Press ; Dragoon : Amerind Foundation, 2016. |
    Includes bibliographical references and index. | Companion volume to *Ancient Paquimé and the Casas
    Grandes World*, 2015.
Identifiers: LCCN 2016010448 | ISBN 9780816534012 (pbk. : alk. paper)
Subjects: LCSH: Casas Grandes culture. | Casas Grandes Site (Mexico)
Classification: LCC E99.C23 D57 2016 | DDC 972/.16—dc23 LC record available at https://lccn.loc.
    gov/2016010448

Dedicated to the Joint Casas Grandes Expedition, especially to
Charles C. Di Peso and Eduardo Contreras Sánchez

CONTENTS

CONTENTS

DISCOVERING PAQUIMÉ

INTRODUCTION

LOOKING BACK FORTY YEARS AT THE JOINT CASAS GRANDES EXPEDITION

PAUL E. MINNIS AND MICHAEL E. WHALEN

We can't know what Charles Di Peso was thinking the first morning of the Joint Casas Grandes Expedition (JCGE) as he looked out over the tall mounds of earth that were the remains of the ancient community now known as Paquimé. An experienced archaeologist, Di Peso meticulously planned the project for months and coordinated his excavation methods with staff members of the Instituto Nacional de Antropología e Historia (INAH) and his codirector, Eduardo Contreras Sánchez. Still, how could Di Peso have known that first morning of the JCGE that the work he was about to begin would consume decades of his professional life, result in one of the premier archaeological excavations in the U.S. Southwest and Northwest Mexico (SW/NW), and eventually transform our understanding of regional prehistory?

Casas Grandes may have been one of the first archaeological sites that Spanish explorers described as they entered the farthest northern reaches of the Spanish empire in Latin America. In the mid-1560s, the chronicler of the expedition led by Francisco de Ibarra, Baltasar Obregón, gave us our first description of Paquimé, perhaps no more than 100 years after the site was abandoned.

> There are many houses of great size, strength, and height. They are six and seven stories, with towers and walls like fortresses for protection and defense against the enemies who undoubtedly used to make war on its inhabitants. The houses contain large and magnificent patios paved with enormous and beautiful stones resembling jasper. There are knife-shaped stones which support the wonderful and big pillars of heavy timbers brought from far away. The walls of the houses were whitewashed and painted in many colors and shades with pictures of the buildings. The structures had some kind of adobe walls. However, it was mixed and interspersed with stone and wood, this combination being stronger and more durable than boards.

During the intervening centuries between Obregón's visit and the start of the JCGE, the brightly colored walls, massive pillars, and fortress-like room blocks were reduced to the tall mounds of earth that Di Peso contemplated on that morning of September 30, 1958—his first day of fieldwork at Paquimé. Fourteen years later, following three years of fieldwork and over a decade of laboratory analysis and write-up, an important new chapter in SW/NW archaeology would be written, and our knowledge of late prehispanic dynamics in this region would be transformed.

PAQUIMÉ: A MAGNIFICENT ANCIENT COMMUNITY

Investigations of the JCGE documented 1,000–2,000 rooms that may have housed over 2,000 people during the Casas Grandes Medio Period between A.D. 1150/1200 and 1450/1475. The many thick, almost concrete-hard walls were

Figure I.1. Aerial view looking south of Paquimé just before JCGE's excavations. The standing walls are from historic structures. There was no way for Di Peso and Contreras to anticipate the extraordinary finds awaiting their research.

Figure I.2. Aerial view looking south of Paquimé just after excavations. Note the unexcavated areas. The JCGE's work at Paquimé and other sites was one of the largest and most complex archaeological projects of its day and remains the largest collaborative archaeological project between Mexico and the United States in the borderlands.

Figure I.3. Workers excavating Paquimé.

Figure I.4. Workers excavating Paquimé. Massive amounts of deposits were removed to reveal the remains of this prehispanic community. Both mechanized equipment and delicate human excavation techniques were used during the three years of fieldwork.

Figure I.5. Charles Di Peso (left foreground, right background) with his wife, Francis Di Peso (right foreground), and other staff members analyzing artifacts at the Amerind Foundation.

made of rammed earth, with massive beams spanning rooms that were, on average, far larger than the typical pueblo rooms of the northern SW/ NW. Unlike their Pueblo neighbors to the north, who built rectangular living and storage spaces, the domestic rooms of Paquimé were typically L-shaped, with a large living area attached to a smaller alcove for sleeping and storage. Other rooms at Paquimé were eccentrically shaped, with many walls (one room had seventeen walls!).

Everything about Paquimé was overbuilt, and the concentration and diversity of ritual architecture attest to its importance as a regional center. Two Mesoamerican-style, I-shaped ball courts were found at Paquimé; these were two of the three largest ball courts in all of northern Chihuahua (a third, much smaller ball court, was excavated in the plaza of a room block). Geometric and animal-shaped platform mounds were common at Paquimé—Di Peso documented a total of fifteen—but were rare in outlying areas, where only one platform mound is known. Other ritually important spaces included rooms with interior shrines and a unique "walk-in" well. In addition, excavations at Paquimé exposed five enormous earth ovens, one of which could have cooked up to 3,000 kg (6,600 lb) of carbohydrate-rich agave (century plant) or other foodstuff. Residents likely used these ovens to prepare food for feasts, perhaps in conjunction with rituals centered on the many platform mounds and ball courts at the site.

Not surprising for farmers in an arid environment, water was of practical and symbolic importance to the people of Paquimé. Paquimé is located along a portion of the Casas Grandes River where the floodplain widens to produce hundreds of acres of arable farmland. Five kilometers north of Paquimé, water from the Ojo Varaleño spring was brought by canal to a large reservoir that supplied domestic water to the community's homes via smaller ditches that snaked through the room blocks. The reservoir and water canals provided a dependable water source that almost certainly impressed the many visitors to the town.

A community the size of Paquimé, occupied for several hundred years, produced and discarded tens of thousands of artifacts: ground stone metates and manos, pottery vessels, and flaked stone tools and tool-making debris. In addition to utilitarian objects, Paquimé's deposits yielded vast quantities of special and exotic artifacts, including 1.5 tons of marine shell (mostly from a few rooms), hundreds of artifacts manufactured from native copper, and perhaps most impressive of all, the remains of hundreds of scarlet and military macaws and the special cages where they were raised and bred. Most of these remains and nonlocal artifacts had their origins in the south and west: macaws from far to the south in Mexico, and shell and copper from the west coast of Mexico. Di Peso and his crew also recovered special goods of closer origin, including turquoise and other minerals.

Interpretations of the role of these special artifacts have changed through time. Di Peso saw them as clear evidence of intense trade and interaction with Mesoamerica. For Di Peso, Paquimé was a major trading center linking Mesoamerica with its vast northwestern frontier. More recent interpretations take a more prosaic view, emphasizing the role of exotic material culture in elaborate and ever-changing rituals that perhaps validated an emergent hierarchy at Paquimé. According to these interpretations, some exotic goods were used as symbols for ritual-political leaders, while others were used as offerings during ceremonies.

Who were these leaders, and how did they lead? Di Peso suggested that the rulers were Mesoamerican traders, known as *pochteca*, who established Paquimé as a trading center to exploit the resources of the vast SW/NW, which Di Peso called Gran Chichimeca. Current views favor the rise of local leaders, but scholars disagree about how they ruled. Some emphasize leadership based on the control of ritual knowledge; others stress the rise of elites who controlled important economic resources. Whatever the source of their power and influence, elites at Paquimé were accorded special treatment when they died. Special grave offerings

accompany some interments at Paquimé, and some elites were buried in specially prepared tombs constructed in ritual architecture.

So Paquimé was home to a large community of people who went about their daily lives in much the same way as their more rural Chihuahuan neighbors. But Paquimé was also an important ritual center that, during its heyday in the thirteenth through fifteenth centuries, was perhaps every bit as impressive as Chaco Canyon and the classic Hohokam centers in New Mexico and Arizona to the north, Cerro de Trincheras in northern Sonora to the west, and La Ferrería in the state of Durango to the south.

A LASTING LEGACY

The JCGE opened the door to our understanding of an important region of the SW/NW, the borderlands of northern Mexico, and the southwestern United States. In addition to excavating at Paquimé, Di Peso and colleagues excavated

Figure I.6. Overview of excavated room blocks. Looking south, this photograph shows the large and compact room blocks and plazas that formed the residential core of Paquimé.

Figure I.7. (right) Reconstruction showing the large room size and massive construction. The average room size at Paquimé was far larger than at contemporary nearby sites. The size of construction required special techniques to support the often-multistoried room blocks. (Photo courtesy of Paul Minnis.)

Figure I.8. (below) Example of a multiple-walled room. While not unique, this room is unusually complicated. The typical room at Paquimé is L shaped.

Figure I.9. A geometric platform mound. Up to 15 platform mounds were constructed at Paquimé. Some are geometric, and others are in the shape of animals. The number of mounds at Paquimé contrasts with only one known platform mound from the hundreds of neighboring communities in the Casas Grandes world.

Figure I.10. Ball court 1 (and associated architectural features) is one of the two large ball courts at Paquimé. We do not know what exact events took place at these ball courts, but they probably were similar to the ball games so widespread in Mesoamerica and northern Mexico.

Figure I.11. The largest earthen oven in the SW/NW was likely used to feed participants during large ritual events held at Paquimé. Nearly 3,000 kg (6,600 lb) of agave or other foodstuffs could have been cooked in this oven.

Figure I.12. The walk-in well. This feature was originally thought to be a source of water. Most scholars now believe it was a water shrine.

Figure I.13. Ojo Varaleño, a large and very dependable spring or seep, provided water to Paquimé and continues to be used by modern-day Casas Grandes. (Photo courtesy of Paul Minnis.)

Figure I.14. One of the two large reservoirs at Paquimé that received water from Ojo Varaleño. While a source for domestic use, the conspicuous water features in such a central location reflect how symbolically important water was to this agricultural community.

Figure I.15. Canals snaking through the room blocks brought water to the community. In addition to bringing water, small canals also took water away from the adobe walls.

sites dating before and after the Medio Period, and they conducted surveys in the mountains and river valleys of northwestern Chihuahua.

Today, we are witnessing a renaissance in Chihuahuan archaeology, with ongoing archaeological projects directed by scholars from Mexico, the United States, and Canada. Some of these projects focus on the Medio Period, when Paquimé reached its apogee, while others study earlier and later time periods to gain as full an understanding as possible of events and processes leading up to the earlier Medio Period and later the decline and abandonment of Paquimé in the fifteenth century.

The United Nations recognized the cultural and historical significance of Paquimé by designating it as a UNESCO World Heritage site in 1996. Visitors to Paquimé can now learn about the history of the site and its excavations at a world-class museum that INAH constructed adjacent to the ruins. None of this would have been possible, of course, without the pioneering research of Charles Di Peso, Eduardo Contreras Sánchez, and their colleagues from INAH and the Amerind Foundation. The purpose of this book is to celebrate that legacy and summarize recent research in northwestern Chihuahua.

Each chapter in this book summarizes recent research that expands our understanding and appreciation of Paquimé, its region, and its role in the prehispanic SW/NW. A more detailed technical volume, *Ancient Paquimé and the Casas Grandes World*, is for those who want to read further. These two publications follow in the path-breaking organization of the eight-volume JCGE report, *Casas Grandes: A Fallen Trading Center of the Gran Chichimeca*. Like the first three volumes of the JCGE report, this book is an easily accessible summary. The last five volumes of the JCGE report provide more detailed documentation and tabular summaries of data, a tradition we emulate in *Ancient Paquimé and the Casas Grandes World*.

1

BEGINNINGS

THE VIEJO PERIOD

MICHAEL T. SEARCY AND JANE H. KELLEY

Farming peoples thrived in the mountains, basins, and river valleys of northwestern Chihuahua for hundreds of years prior to the construction of platform mounds and ball courts at Paquimé. Their small pithouse villages dotted the landscape near the rich floodplain of the Casas Grandes River, where they farmed maize, beans, and other foods. It was during this time (A.D. 400–1200), known as the Viejo Period, that the foundations of the Chihuahuan culture were formed.

While recognized as forming the roots of a more complex society, Viejo Period sites lack the monumental architecture and ornate pottery of the Medio Period (A.D. 1150/1200–1450/1475), which have attracted archaeologists and tourists to the region for decades. One reason Viejo Period sites are understudied is that many are virtually invisible because they are buried under the adobe mounds of later inhabitants and appear as little more than scatters of artifacts on the ground surface. Some of the first clues into this earlier era were unearthed in the excavations of Charles Di Peso at the Convento Site. Conducting test excavations in a seventeenth-century Spanish settlement a few kilometers north of Casas Grandes, Di Peso discovered a cluster of underlying Viejo Period dwellings that were almost a thousand years older than the Spanish occupation.

As Di Peso and his crew worked to uncover the remains of these older houses, they found evidence of three superimposed villages. The earliest villages, comprising Di Peso's Convento phase

(A.D. 700–900) and Pilón phase (A.D. 900–950), were clusters of shallow semicircular pithouses with jacal (pole, brush, and adobe) walls. This technique of house construction was similar to early pithouse forms in other cultures of the prehispanic North American West, including the Ancestral Pueblo, Hohokam, Mimbres, and Fremont. By the middle of the tenth century (Di Peso's Perros Bravos phase, A.D. 950–1200), pithouses had given way to aboveground, rectilinear, adobe-walled rooms. The reason for this shift is unknown, although in other parts of the SW/NW the transition to surface rooms coincided with an increase in residential stability. Clear evidence for the transition to aboveground rooms has yet to be clearly documented in other parts of northern Chihuahua.

Di Peso's excavations at the Convento Site provided our first and one of our last glimpses of pre–Medio Period archaeology in northwestern Chihuahua. Although Di Peso excavated parts of two other Viejo Period sites, in the fifty years since the Joint Casas Grandes Expedition few Viejo Period sites have been excavated and analyzed. As a result, for over half a century, Di Peso's interpretations of the Viejo Period stood unchanged and unchallenged. Fortunately, recent work in southern Chihuahua by Jane Kelley and her colleagues has shed new light on Di Peso's foundational work and challenged some of his interpretations.

Kelley's excavations at the Calderon Site in southern Chihuahua uncovered several

Figure 1.1. Aerial view of JCGE's excavation of a Viejo Period pithouse village at the Convento Site a few kilometers north of Paquimé. Research at this site provided information about times both earlier and later than the Medio Period. The Convento Site is open to the public.

Figure 1.2. A large pithouse at the Convento site is interpreted as a ritual structure. Research at this site provides the foundation of what we know about the Viejo Period.

Figure 1.3. Excavations at the Calderon Site, a Viejo Period site south of the Casas Grandes heartland. Excavation at this site has greatly expanded understanding of the Viejo Period. (Photo courtesy of Jane Kelley.)

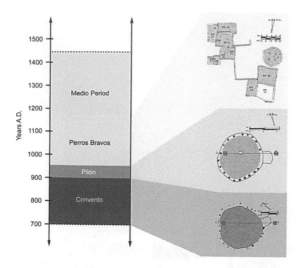

Figure 1.4. Viejo Period timeline and associated architectural styles. As with areas to the north, there was a transition from pithouses to aboveground rooms. (Image courtesy of Michael Searcy.)

superimposed pithouses, and using ground-penetrating radar, Kelley found evidence of another twenty-nine pit structures at the Calderon Site, making it somewhat larger than the Convento Site. Viejo Period architecture at the Calderon Site is not as consistent as architecture at the Convento Site. Although pithouses were round and covered with adobe, there was not much evidence for walls built with closely spaced wooden poles, like those found at the Convento Site. Instead, inhabitants built up adobe around the base of the pit wall, and large wooden posts set in the floors of the houses helped support the roof.

Based on these explorations and others, archaeologists have been able to reconstruct some general patterns of Viejo Period culture and lifeways. Viejo Period residents often built their villages near major watercourses, along primary rivers in the well-watered valleys to the north, and along rivers and secondary streams in the south. Often situated on terraces, villages overlooked prime farmland on river floodplains. The Viejo people were subsistence farmers who grew maize, beans, and squash. But they also foraged for wild foods, such as walnuts, goosefoot, and amaranth, and they hunted bison, jackrabbits, duck, and turkey to complement their maize diet.

Excavations have also brought to light many of the manufactured goods made by Viejo Period people. They produced brownware pottery that was plain, textured, or decorated with red geometric designs. These vessels ranged in size from 7.6 to 19 liters (2–5 gal) and were likely used for cooking and storing water and food. In addition to locally produced ceramics, Mimbres Black-on-white pottery has been found on sites that date to the later part of the Viejo Period (ca. A.D. 1000), which shows that the Viejo people not only were aware of their northern neighbors but also engaged in active trade relations with them.

In addition to pottery, copper artifacts and marine shell were traded from as far away as the west coast of Mexico. Trade in marine shell played a prominent role in the lives of Medio Period artisans and traders, but, based on an abundance of *Glycymeris*, *Nassarius*, and *Olivella* shell bracelets and bead jewelry, the shell trade was important in earlier periods as well. While sites during the Medio Period, specifically Paquimé, boast nearly 4,000,000 pieces of marine shell, the more active trade routes of this later era were likely started in the Viejo Period.

In an astonishing discovery of an infant burial at the Calderon Site, excavators found over 800 pieces of marine shell along with an elaborately constructed pendant with inlaid stone in the form of a cross. The presence of a highly adorned infant burial provides tantalizing evidence of hereditary status during the Viejo Period and suggests that kin groups began to sort themselves into ranked hierarchies—a prelude, perhaps, to the social ranking evident during the later Medio Period. Much lies undiscovered beneath the soil in northwestern Chihuahua, and many basic questions remain unanswered about the earliest foundations of Paquimé culture: When did the Viejo Period begin? What was the size of the Viejo population? How many different types of structures did they build, and do those structures correspond with different periods of time? Did people experiment with the domestication of animals such as macaws and turkeys? Why did people move from pithouses to aboveground adobe buildings? What was the nature of their long-distance relationships with other groups to the north or with places like the west coast? How did the Viejo Period lay the

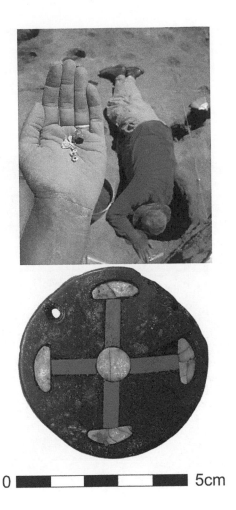

Figure 1.5. Excavation of an infant burial that yielded a surprisingly large number of grave offerings, including this exquisite pendant. (Photo courtesy of Jane Kelley.)

foundations for the growth and expansion of Paquimé during the thirteenth and fourteenth centuries? In archaeology, questions almost always outnumber answers, but as archaeologists continue to search for these explanations, our knowledge will grow exponentially. What we do know is that during the Viejo Period, farmers settled down in villages and thrived in a difficult arid environment. Agriculture, trade, and architectural proficiency were all well established long before the start of the Medio Period in A.D. 1150/1200s. And while their numbers were likely smaller and less stratified than during the Medio Period, the Viejo Period people of Chihuahua sowed the seeds that future generations would use to build one of the greatest and most culturally rich centers in the SW/NW.

Figure 2.1. The especially wide and fertile floodplain near Paquimé, which is in the background. The ability to produce food surpluses may have helped emergent leaders build their power base.

2

ECOLOGY AND FOOD ECONOMY

PAUL E. MINNIS AND MICHAEL E. WHALEN

Paquimé was an important political, social, and ritual center containing over a ton of shell, hundreds of scarlet macaw skeletons, large ball courts, platform mounds, and massive room blocks, but it was also a community with thousands of people going about their daily lives. If we are to understand those lives and their histories, we need to look beyond the monuments and sumptuary artifacts to the ecology and economy of the Paquimé people and their neighbors. How did they farm their semiarid homeland? What crops did they grow? How did they supplement the products of their fields with wild plant and animal resources? Did they practice animal husbandry beyond raising parrots and turkeys? How did the subsistence economy articulate with the economy of ritual and political power? Were crop surpluses used by aspiring leaders in their quest to gain power and influence?

All people of the SW/NW used the environmental diversity of their desert and mountain homeland to broaden their economic opportunities. To the west of Paquimé is the Sierra Madre Occidental, the massive continental mountain range clothed in conifer forests, incised by verdant river valleys, and dotted with the homesteads of prehispanic farmers. To the east are the extensive semidesert plains, grasslands, and dunes of northwestern Chihuahua, a desolate landscape with few permanent village sites but a region offering extensive opportunities for hunting and gathering. Paquimé is located in the Casas Grandes River valley, with its perennial stream that originates in the high Sierra Madre and

so provides a predictable flow of water and especially abundant fertile soil for farming. Streams and river valleys like the Casas Grandes, with their arable floodplains and high-altitude watersheds, supported the vast majority of prehispanic farmers in northwestern Chihuahua.

It is hardly a coincidence that Paquimé grew to its great size at a place where the Casas Grandes River floodplain expands to provide over 2,000 ha (nearly 5,000 ac) of arable land. The Casas Grandes River floodplain begins to widen just upstream from Paquimé, and the gentle topography of the floodplain's eastern edge may have permitted farmers to expand their fields beyond the natural floodplain to open up even more arable acres. Medio Period farmers, like most indigenous farmers of the SW/NW, planted maize in most of their fields, but they also grew beans, squash, gourds, cotton, agave, and chile. The discovery of chile is especially noteworthy, as the chile remains recently found at two sites near Paquimé along the Casas Grandes River floodplain are the only cultivated chile found thus far in the SW/NW before the arrival of the Spaniards (contradicting the impression that "southwestern" cuisine has always been spicy!). Plant remains retrieved from archaeological sites next to lowland floodplain settings indicate that they grew more cotton and beans than sites in upland settings.

The abundant arable land at Paquimé suggests that residents of Chihuahua's largest community may have been able to produce sizeable

Figure 2.2. River valleys in the mountains west of Paquimé were important settlement locations. (Photo courtesy of Paul Minnis.)

Figure 2.3. Although not as visually spectacular as the mountains, the widespread plains of northern Chihuahua provided important foods and minerals for the ancient people of the Casas Grandes world. (Photo courtesy of Paul Minnis.)

Figure 2.4. Agricultural terraces dot the foothills around Paquimé and offered residents alternative farming settings to the floodplains. Hundreds of such fields are known from northwestern Chihuahua. (Photo courtesy of Paul Minnis and Michael Whalen.)

Figure 2.5. Mesquite pods. The carbohydrate-rich fruits were an important food. The resin was a valued adhesive, and the wood was an excellent fuel source. (Photo courtesy of Paul Minnis.)

food surpluses that could have been used to fuel periodic feasts that lubricated regional friendships and alliances and perhaps supported a class of "elite" non-food producers as well. As mentioned before, one of the earth ovens excavated at Paquimé was large enough to have processed over 3,000 kg of food, an indication, perhaps, of the size of some of the feasts held at Paquimé.

There is little doubt that lowland floodplain farming produced the highest yields practiced by the people of prehispanic Chihuahua and were the most dependable of all agriculture. However, traditional farmers around the world rarely use only one farming strategy. Instead, they minimize their risk by planting their crops in multiple field locations. It is especially important for floodwater farmers to develop alternative field locations as insurance against unpredictable flood events that can destroy entire field systems. Residents of Paquimé and their neighbors were clearly attuned to such risks. Many slopes around Paquimé and in the Sierra Madre to the west were sculpted with series of low stone walls to create level farming terraces. Terraces not only provide a level surface to plant crops but also help slow down runoff and help retain moisture after storms. We know that maize and agave were grown in upland terrace fields, but a variety of other crops could have been grown there as well.

Most agricultural terraces in northwestern Chihuahua are small, about the size that a single family might have constructed and farmed. A few,

Figure 2.6. A flowering agave (mescal or century plant). Agave was an important food source and likely was cultivated widely around Paquimé and other areas of the SW/NW. (Photo courtesy Paul Minnis.)

however, are far larger, and these tend to be located near sites that archaeologists believe served as special ritual or administrative centers. One hypothesis is that these large fields were constructed and maintained by community members to serve the needs of ritual leaders or chiefs. If this hypothesis is correct, the harvest from these fields might have gone toward ritual feasts that would have provided food for the whole community and, at the same time, enhanced the status of the leaders.

HUNTING AND GATHERING

Traditional farmers also make use of naturally occurring plants for food, fuel, medicine, and construction, and the study of plant remains from archaeological sites in northwestern Chihuahua has documented the use of dozens of wild plants. Of particular importance to the people of Chihuahua were mesquite pods, pine nuts, acorns, native agaves and sotol, and various species of cacti. The seeds of common garden weeds were also important in the diet. Plants such as goosefoot, pigweed, and purslane thrive on the margins of active and fallow fields and would have provided edible greens in the spring and nutritious seeds in the summer. With the dense population of farming communities during the Medio Period in the Casas Grandes region, weeds would have found many favorable habitats and would have been collected wherever they grew. Wood for construction and fuel was also an important resource and would likely have entailed forays into the nearby Sierra Madre after local sources were depleted.

The people of Paquimé are justifiably famous for their husbandry of macaws and turkeys. What is perhaps less known is that these birds were raised for ritual sacrifice, not for food. The people of Paquimé obtained all of their meat from wild animals. Desert rabbits were a major food source, as indicated by the quantity of rabbit bones in Medio Period trash deposits (Villa Ahumada, a contemporary community east of Paquimé, is famous for its abundance of rabbit bones). Rabbits and other animals would have been attracted to the agricultural fields of northwestern Chihuahua and could

easily have been hunted close to home. For larger game such as deer, forays into the nearby Sierra Madre would have provided much larger packages of meat.

Di Peso believed that bison was an important food item because bison bones constitute a large percentage of the overall bone count from Paquimé. Unfortunately, excavations of the Joint Casas Grandes Expedition occurred before quarter-inch and smaller screens were routinely used to sift for small artifacts such as rabbit and other small animal bones, so the significance of large animal bones as a fraction of the overall bone assemblage at Paquimé is difficult to evaluate. This doesn't mean that Di Peso was wrong about the importance of bison and other large game animals. It simply means that he may not have appreciated the relative importance of small animals in the diet at Paquimé. Subsequent excavations suggest that the bones of large animals may be more abundant at special sites that served as administrative or ritual centers. While most people of the Paquimé world probably obtained the majority of their meat from small animals like rabbits, more desirable meats such as bison were likely more accessible to elite leaders and for special events at special sites such as Paquimé.

Paquimé was more than its fancy artifacts. Its well-being clearly depended on the fruits from its fields, forests, plains, mountains, and rivers. By all accounts, these resources were abundant and dependable. The majestic community of Paquimé and its wealth would have drawn visitors from throughout northwestern Chihuahua and beyond. But did the large Medio Period population of Paquimé eventually have a deleterious effect on the local environment? There is some evidence for the depletion of fuel wood supplies around large sites and, not surprisingly, the increase—along with population—of weeds and other plants adapted to disturbed soils. It is unlikely that many deer or antelope freely ranged around Paquimé during its heyday. As local population increased, hunters probably had to range farther afield in search of big game. Did local resource depletion play a role in Paquimé's decline in the fifteenth century? Perhaps future research can address this question.

3

ASSEMBLY LINES OR HANDICRAFTS

HOW THINGS WERE MADE AT PAQUIMÉ

GORDON F. M. RAKITA AND RAFAEL CRUZ ANTILLÓN

Many visitors to the ancient ruins at Paquimé are understandably impressed by the enormous size of the site, the breadth of the walls, the size of the colossal wooden beams, and the variety of different rooms, platform mounds, ball courts, and other structures. It is no wonder that the site earned the name Casas Grandes. But if Paquimé were simply a big empty site, then it would not have attracted so much attention from archaeologists and the general public. Equally intriguing are the things that were found in and around the community's ruins. Richly painted pottery vessels, turquoise beads, copper bells, turkeys, macaws, and rooms full of vast quantities of shells—these are the things that make all of us gape in astonishment. Understanding how these various commodities were produced and used is an important part of shedding light on the lifeways of the ancient Paquiméans.

How a society makes and uses the things people need and want can tell us a great deal about

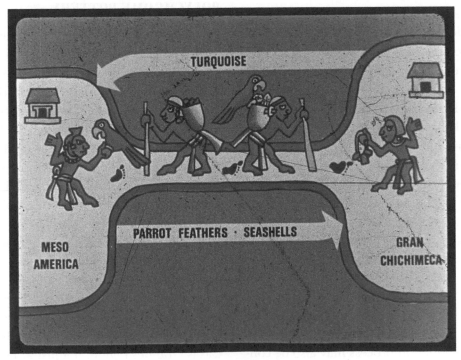

Figure 3.1. An illustration of Di Peso's model of long-distance trade between Mesoamerica and the SW/NW. He suggested that Paquimé's role was a major note in southwestern/Mesoamerican trade that led to its rise and widespread influence.

that society. Communities in which each house-hold produces and consumes all of the commodi-ties required to maintain itself are different from communities where different households produce different commodities and thus are dependent upon each other for needed items. Likewise, soci-eties that produce more of a craft item than they need and exchange that item with other societies are linked into trade networks. So understanding

Figure 3.2. An example of Ramos Polychrome, the signature painted pottery from the Medio Period. These vessels are often decorated with religiously important images.

how things are produced, traded, used, and ulti-mately discarded can tell us much about the day-to-day lives of people who lived over 800 years ago.

How do archaeologists reconstruct how things were made in ancient times? How do we distin-guish household production from the production of craft specialists and from large-scale assembly line production? The most direct evidence of craft production consists of the tools used in the produc-tion process and production debris—the discarded residues of the production process. The clustering of raw materials, debris, and production tools in a location within a site provides clues to where things were made. The total number of objects found at a site may give clues to how things were produced and used. Large quantities of one item might be the result of trading, stockpiling, or per-haps a massive local production effort. Clues to the nature of the production process may also be con-tained in the objects themselves. We are all famil-iar with the carbon-copy nature of mass-produced

consumer goods. In contrast, objects produced by individual craftspeople in different workshops tend to exhibit variation in design and workman-ship. Archaeologists look at all of these lines of evidence when they try to reconstruct how people used and produced objects in the past. Charles Di Peso and his collaborators on the Joint Casas Grandes Expedition (JCGE) were the first to examine the manufacture of goods at Paquimé. Di Peso interpreted the archaeological evidence as an indication of an expansive, well-organized, large-scale commodity production system unrivaled in the prehispanic SW/NW. Many archaeologists who have come after Di Peso have interpreted the evidence differently. Most have acknowledged the impressive craft goods found at Paquimé, but they see a much less elaborate system of manufacture. Here, we focus on some key craft items that have attracted the most attention of Casas Grandes scholars: shell, turquoise, copper, and polychrome pottery. We also address the role that macaws and turkeys may have played in the economy of Paquimé.

POLYCHROME POTTERY

No objects associated with Paquimé attract more attention from both the public and scholars than the thousands of beautiful polychrome pottery vessels recovered from Paquimé and nearby sites. Di Peso's crews found large quantities of whole and broken polychrome vessels at Paquimé, and the distinctively painted pottery is found through-out much of northern Chihuahua, southern New Mexico, and parts of Arizona and Sonora. Raw lumps of clay, unfired clay coils, polishing stones, sherd scrapers, and a "firing wad" were found at Paquimé, all of which suggest that pottery pro-duction took place within the city. However, no specific kiln area for pottery firing was identified during Di Peso's excavations. Various chemical analyses of Chihuahuan polychrome sherds indi-cate that the pottery was made throughout the Casas Grandes region, not just at Paquimé, which suggests a level of production at Paquimé sim-ilar to that of other prehispanic communities in the region. It remains unknown, however, where Paquimé's artisans fired their pots.

SHELL

In total, the JCGE recovered nearly 4,000,000 pieces of shell from Paquimé, including both worked and unworked pieces. Marine shell from the west coast of Mexico dominates the assemblage, but there are also freshwater and land species represented. The vast majority (over 95 percent) of the shell objects at Paquimé were beads made from a marine snail, *Nassarius* species, by the very simple process of poking a hole in the shell. Perforation of *Nassarius* shells would have been a simple task, requiring little if any specialized knowledge, elaborate tools, or physical effort. Significantly, however, there is little evidence that shells were perforated at Paquimé. Instead, evidence indicates that the shells were probably brought from western Mexico as strings of finished

beads, which contradicts Di Peso's hypothesis that shell working was a major industry at Paquimé. The vast quantity of shell recovered at Paquimé suggests that they were an important commodity, and the fact that shell ornaments comprised the majority of grave goods at Paquimé bolsters their importance as a major item of exotic trade.

TURQUOISE

The amount and location of turquoise recovered at Paquimé combined with the lack of significant turquoise production debris suggest that Paquimé was mostly a consumer of turquoise objects, just as it was mostly a consumer of marine shell. Excavations revealed nearly 6,000 pieces of turquoise weighing almost 1.5 kg (3 lb) at Paquimé. However, most of the turquoise at Paquimé was found in a single ceremonial cache placed at the bottom of one of the water reservoirs. Thus, turquoise was not used by many "consumers" for

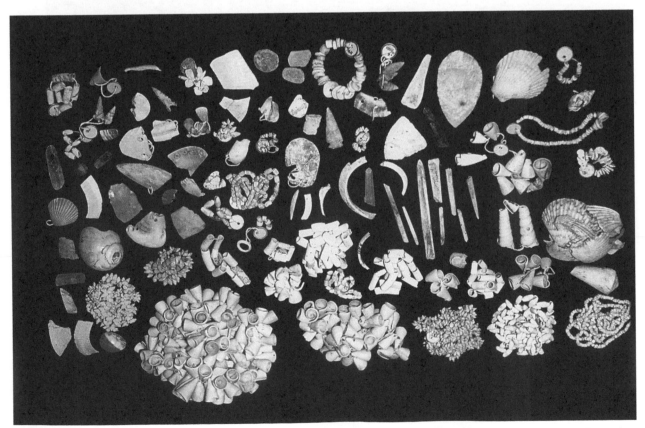

Figure 3.3. The variety of shell recovered from JCGE's excavations at Paquimé is clear evidence of trade with groups to the west. Most shell artifacts from Paquimé, however, were simple beads.

Figure 3.4. Most of the shell came from a few rooms, such as this one in Unit 8 being excavated. In addition to the shell, most mineral specimens and 50 pots were found in this room.

Figure 3.5. A jar of turquoise buried as an offering under a reservoir. Turquoise was not as abundant at Paquimé as at other regional centers in the SW/NW, such as Chaco Canyon.

Figure 3.6. A collection of copper artifacts. These artifacts came from western Mexico, and few if any were made at Paquimé.

personal adornment. Although the tools that could have been used to work turquoise are abundant and widespread at Paquimé, the lack of significant amounts of production debris in the form of waste pieces suggests that working turquoise was not a major activity at the site. Other sites east of Paquimé provide far better evidence for production of finished turquoise objects.

COPPER

Crews also recovered over 600 copper artifacts during excavations at Paquimé. Although this is an unusually large amount of copper from one site, excavations at Paquimé found no evidence of furnaces or special tools that would indicate copper smelting, so it is doubtful that the people of Paquimé were advanced metallurgists. To the contrary, much of the copper was probably traded into Paquimé from the west coast of Mexico along trade routes that paralleled most of the marine shell at Paquimé. The facts that copper objects were not manufactured at the site and that most were recovered from nonmortuary ritual contexts suggest that an elite subset of the population exercised control over these items once they reached Paquimé.

MACAWS

An astonishing number of macaws were discovered at Paquimé: 322 scarlet macaws, an additional 81 military macaws, and 100 macaws of undetermined species. Fifty-six nesting pens with macaw remains and feces were also uncovered, along with 125 stone ring doorways and 95 nesting door plugs. Chemical analyses of macaw bones from Paquimé indicate that many of the birds were born and raised at the site (though several samples indicate possible importation). Thus, it seems that the ancient Paquiméans not only imported these tropical birds but also maintained a breeding population. As already mentioned, there is no evidence that people ate macaws. People apparently raised macaws for their brilliant feathers, which still figure prominently in SW/NW ceremonies,

and they sacrificed them as part of some long-forgotten ritual.

Figure 3.7. A scarlet macaw, with its magnificent multicolored plumage, may well be the most impressive remains from Paquimé. These skeletons of birds are far more common at Paquimé than any other site in the SW/NW. (Photo courtesy of Paul Minnis.)

TURKEYS

Excavators uncovered the remains of 344 turkeys and many roosting pens at Paquimé. Over 60 percent of the birds recovered were fully articulated and intentionally buried, but without heads. Their lack of heads makes a strong case that ritual participants used turkeys as sacrifices. Turkey remains are found in prehispanic sites throughout the SW/NW, where their feathers were used as insulation and in rituals and their meat was sometimes consumed, and turkeys are notoriously easy to domesticate. Thus, there is no reason to believe that Paquimé was a production center for distribution of turkeys over a wide region, as it almost certainly was for macaws. It is unclear whether turkey husbandry at Paquimé was a short-lived, high-intensity event or an effort that occurred at a low but sustained rate for a long period, as both possibilities would likely produce the same archaeological traces. Presumably, everyone would have had the necessary raw materials to raise turkeys, yet turkey remains tend to be concentrated in certain portions of the site, which suggests centralized control of these ritually important birds and their feathers.

CONCLUSIONS

Di Peso's supposition that production at Paquimé was organized by specialized craft guilds rather clearly evolved from his belief that Paquimé was a large commercial trading center. A critical review

of the evidence, however, suggests that craft manufacturing at Paquimé resembled production patterns at many other communities in the SW/NW. Many types of objects such as pottery and perhaps turkeys were likely made and raised by members of individual households. When it comes to nonlocal commodities such as shell, turquoise, and copper, it appears that Paquimé was principally a consumer rather than manufacturer or middleman trader. Turquoise was probably acquired in finished form from areas to the north and east, while shell and copper almost certainly came from the west Mexican coast. Macaws were also probably originally acquired from Mexico, though at some point the Paquiméans developed a breeding population to supply their needs, which probably included the trade of feathers for other sumptuary goods. Each of these nonlocal objects was probably ritually important and may have figured in long-distance trade with other groups.

Figure 3.8. A plaza with macaw pens. This is the best-preserved macaw-raising area, with pens and associated tools to maintain these animals.

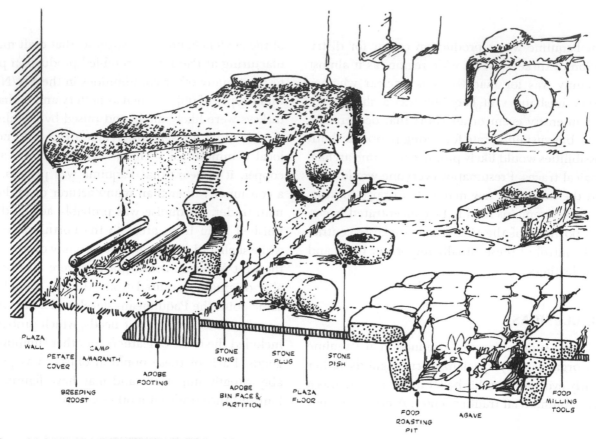

Figure 3.9. Interpretive diagram of macaw-raising area.

Figure 3.10. The plaza with many turkey pens, the remains of which are stub walls attached to the plaza walls. Turkeys may have been as symbolically important as macaws.

4

SERPENTS FROM SKY TO WATER

CASAS GRANDES RELIGION AND LEADERS

CHRISTINE S. VANPOOL AND TODD L. VANPOOL

Water was the most vital resource for ancient farmers. Without it, crops withered and died in the dry environment. So it is not unusual that Casas Grandes religious imagery focused on water. Feathered serpent imagery is the prime example. Across the Americas, the feathered (or at times horned) serpents are supernatural entities that control water. The Aztecs' Quetzalcóatl was a feathered rattlesnake that flew through the air to herd clouds and bring rain. The feathered serpent of Zuni Pueblo in western New Mexico is Ko'loowisi, who lives in the watery underworld. He watches humans from springs and rewards good behavior with nice gentle rains and fertile crops. He punishes bad behavior with lightning strikes, drought, and catastrophic rains that cause crops to wash away. Other Puebloans have similar water serpents that go by different names.

The Paquimé horned/feathered serpent fits within the larger plumed serpent tradition. Polychrome pots often depict the feathered serpent, as does rock art found around springs. On pottery, the serpent is often depicted as a whole snake complete with a head, body, and tail and more abstractly as just the serpent's head. Skilled potters sometimes painted the serpent as a head-dress that men wore while conducting ceremonies. Perhaps the most impressive representation of the plumed serpent is the Mound of the Serpent at Paquimé. The mound, 113 m (371 ft) long, was a "check dam" that diverted water around the adobe pueblo. It is literally a feathered serpent that controlled water for the community. The serpent's head had an appendage representing a feather or

a horn and two white caliche eyes. The westward eye, which faced away from the community, had a carved Mesoamerican-style image of a plumed serpent. However, this serpent had dorsal feathers attached to its midback, which was not typical of southwestern plumed serpents. (Perhaps he saw another serpent in the sky or in the distance.) Suggesting perhaps that the serpent was keeping a watchful eye on the people, the other eye pointed at the community and was blank.

Charles Di Peso was adamant that the horned serpent was the central deity of the Casas Grandes people, who, he concluded, followed the Mesoamerican serpent tradition associated with Quetzalcóatl. According to Di Peso, priests associated with this deity largely controlled Casas Grandes religion, but they were not alone. There were other "cult institutions" that were

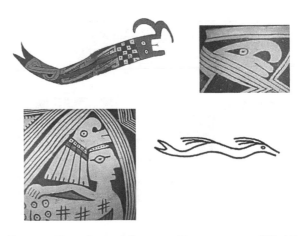

Figure 4.1. Horned serpent depictions. (Images courtesy of Christine VanPool, the Amerind Foundation, and the Centennial Museum at the University of Texas at El Paso, Cat. No. A 36.85.18.)

complementary to, as opposed to antagonistic toward, the worship of the feathered serpent. One of these institutions focused on Tláloc, the Mesoamerican deity that controlled rain. Based on ethnographic and historic analogy, Di Peso proposed that the hundreds of turkey burials he recovered at Paquimé were sacrifices for Tláloc. The decapitated birds received formal burials without being eaten. Ritual participants probably drank the turkeys' blood and used the feathers to adorn headdresses and other sacred objects. Finally, in Mesoamerica the Xipe Tótec complex reigned over "nature's regeneration" through human sacrifices, with priests wearing the skins of flayed humans. Evidence for Xipe's worship at Paquimé includes human sacrifices and human trophy heads, Xipe effigy pots with closed eyes and open mouths, and ritual drinking of the juice of the agave plant.

Another striking feature of Paquimé is the introduction of the Mesoamerican ball game. Typically, teams of four to six participants played this game on a relatively small field about 28 m (92 ft) long. Much like soccer, players could also use their hips. At Paquimé the game was played in three ball courts, complete with viewing areas and high retaining walls. Excavations uncovered a human sacrifice under one of the ball courts. Elsewhere in the region, ball courts were far less elaborate, and some were as simple as flat areas outlined by rocks. Because ball games are associated

Figure 4.2. Males smoking and dancing. The shamanistic transformation was indicated by the # sign. (Images courtesy of Christine VanPool, the Amerind Foundation, and the Centennial Museum at the University of Texas at El Paso, Cat. No. A 36.85.18.)

with Quetzalcóatl in Mesoamerican religion, the courts were likely tied to water-related ritual; but it is also likely that elites used the game to compete with one another and show their dominance.

Figure 4.3. The Casas Grandes spirit world. (Images courtesy of Christine VanPool.)

RELIGION AND LEADERSHIP

The Casas Grandes culture was one of the most politically complex in the greater SW/NW, and it is apparent that elites gained power, at least in part, through their control of religious practices. Di Peso contended that Paquimé's priests of the Quetzalcóatl and other religious complexes controlled public education, trade relationships, economic production, and other aspects of Paquimé life. Michael Whalen and Paul Minnis describe a much less centralized political system at Paquimé, with elites from different communities competing with each other for regional dominance. Archaeologist Gordon Rakita presents a third view. Instead of the specific priestly organizations Di Peso proposes, Rakita sees two distinct religious expressions: (1) the Earth Fertility cult (stressing group solidarity and environmental rejuvenation); and (2) the Ancestor cult (emphasizing and legitimizing the social differences between farmers/craftsmen and priests/leaders). Each of these cults was associated with different objects and ritual areas. The Ancestor cult's focus on social power was epitomized by the Mound of Offerings at Paquimé. The mound contained the bones (except for the skulls) of two males and a female kept in large pots. Paquiméans ritually removed and manipulated the bodies on occasion, perhaps yearly. Elsewhere at Paquimé, there was a room with limited access containing five trophy skulls, reflecting interaction with the dead, presumably ancestors. With an emphasis on water ritual, the

Earth Fertility cult focused on the serpent imagery previously discussed.

We offer a somewhat different view of Casas Grandes religion. Di Peso distinguished between priests and shamans, and he argued that although both types of practitioners probably existed at Paquimé, organized priesthoods dominated the religious system and, by extension, the political, economic, and educational systems of the community. According to Di Peso, shamans conducted healing and other ceremonies for individuals but were not part of the formal priesthoods or the theocratic political hierarchy. Di Peso's priest/shaman distinction was consistent with the anthropological views of his time, but we think there is evidence to challenge this traditional dichotomy. Anthropologists once thought that shamanism was limited to simple foraging societies, whereas priesthoods emerged in complex societies where the emphasis was on communal rituals and full-time religious specialists. However, archaeologists working with the Maya, Aztec, and other complex Mesoamerican societies have found that priest/leaders directed communal rituals but also engaged in behavior typical of shamans, assuming altered states of consciousness in order to interact with the spirit world. We suspect that Paquimé ritual was directed by similar "shaman priests," and the evidence is in the iconography.

We have observed that Medio Period pottery effigies of males smoking and wearing feathered serpent headdresses tend to be decorated with a very rare symbol similar to a pound sign and that anthropomorphs with either horned heads or macaw heads are often associated with this same symbol. Among the over 5,000 whole Casas Grandes pots that we have examined, the pound sign symbol is limited to the smoking, headdress-wearing individuals and anthropomorphs. We propose that the figures bearing the pound sign reflect shamans who smoked pipes (perhaps filled with *Nicotiana rustica*, a native tobacco that is potent enough to reliably produce visions), danced (reflected by individuals wearing headdresses), and perhaps fasted in order to enter an altered state of consciousness known as a shamanic journey. While in a trance, they presumably interacted with supernatural entities, including the feathered serpent and an indeterminate deity represented as a diamond with two macaw heads. The double-headed Macaw Diamond is commonly depicted on female effigies, indicating some association with women.

We argue further that shaman-priests were tied to leadership in the Casas Grandes region. Shamanic paraphernalia at Paquimé includes cylinder stone pipes identical to those depicted on smoker effigies and small copper bells. It also includes quartz and other minerals that were present in a ritually central area of Paquimé along with a very large jar decorated with shaman figures. These shaman-priests may be related to the religious institutions Di Peso and Rakita have proposed. The emphasis on the plumed serpent (Quetzalcóatl) naturally suggests that the shaman-priests were linked to that particular deity.

The Casas Grandes religious system focused on elite priesthoods that were both politically and religiously powerful. Casas Grandes shaman-priests smoked the native tobacco, danced in richly adorned feathered headdresses, and communed with powerful spirits such as the feathered serpent. They integrated aspects of Mesoamerican religious systems that included playing the Mesoamerican ball game, worshiping deities such as Quetzalcóatl and Tláloc, and perhaps even sacrificing human beings to ensure access to water and agricultural productivity. However, their connection with Mesoamerican religious systems should not be overdrawn. There are profound differences between the historically and ethnographically described feathered serpent traditions of Mesoamerica and the SW/NW. Important as the worship of the serpent was, the Casas Grandes ceremonies likely differed from those observed elsewhere. Even the serpent's name was likely unique to whatever language the Paquimé people spoke. Through their social power and rituals, the Casas Grandes shaman-priests helped create one of the most socially complex, artistically distinct, and geographically expansive archaeological traditions in the SW/NW.

5

CASAS GRANDES AND ITS CLOSEST NEIGHBORS

MICHAEL E. WHALEN AND TODD A. PITEZEL

Casas Grandes stands out from contemporary Chihuahuan communities because of its massive architecture and spectacular artifacts. But great centers almost never exist in isolation. They typically interact in complex ways with other contemporary communities. There are hundreds of Medio Period (A.D. 1150/1200–1450/1475) sites from surrounding regions that shared basic cultural patterns with Casas Grandes. How did these communities relate to Casas Grandes? Di Peso believed that Casas Grandes, because of its large size and ritual architecture, exerted

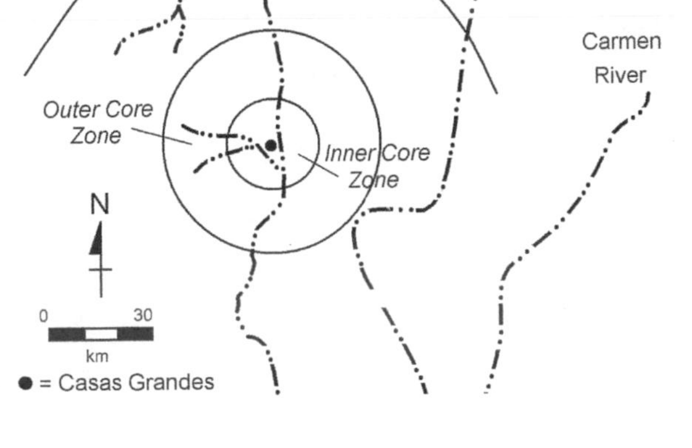

Figure 5.1. A map of the region around Paquimé. (Map courtesy of Michael Whalen.)

political control over a large area. Other researchers, including the present authors, question Casas Grandes' regional hegemony. Fortunately, recent archaeological research has been able to build an empirical basis for evaluating the regional character and influence of Paquimé.

The Medio Period is preceded by the Viejo Period, an early agricultural adaptation in which people lived first in semisubterranean pithouses and later in the surface structures that were the predecessors of Medio Period pueblos. The Viejo settlement pattern is poorly known, but it seems to be composed of fewer and smaller communities than in the succeeding Medio Period. Consequently, the Medio Period seems to have seen significant changes from the preceding Viejo Period. The basic architectural components of Medio communities were blocks of contiguous rooms built of adobe. Medio Period pueblos have been recorded unsystematically since the early 1930s, and a survey project in northwestern Chihuahua located more than 300 of them between 1994 and 1995. Most Medio Period settlements were composed of one to three room blocks, a few had four to five blocks, and there were a few settlements with six or more room blocks. Few if any recorded mounds appear to have been more than one story in height. Despite the presence of a few medium to large sites, the great majority of Medio sites recorded on survey were small, with fewer than ten rooms. Casas Grandes is four times larger than its next largest neighboring Medio Period site, so Paquimé

Figure 5.2. Hundreds of Medio Period communities dot the Casas Grandes world. Archaeologists have found low earthen mounds, which are the remains of collapsed adobe houses. These sites and their artifacts provide clues to the relationships between these hamlets and villages and Paquimé. (Photo courtesy of Michael Whalen and Paul Minnis.)

Figure 5.3. A ball court in the area surrounding Paquimé. None of the outlying ball courts are as large as the two at Paquimé. Regional ball courts are not all the same size and shape. (Photo courtesy of Paul Minnis and Michael Whalen.)

Figure 5.4. A large excavated earthen oven at an outlying site. Like the large ovens at Paquimé, the elaborate ovens in surrounding areas served to prepare food for feasts as a part of events that drew people together. (Photo courtesy of Paul Minnis and Michael Whalen.)

Figure 5.5. A large unexcavated earthen oven. It is like the excavated oven shown in figure 5.4. (Photo courtesy of Michael Whalen and Paul Minnis.)

Figure 5.6. Macaw pen entrance stones at an outlying site 20 km (12 mi) from Paquimé. (Photo courtesy of Michael Whalen and Paul Minnis.)

Figure 5.7. El Pueblito, a special site and ritual center, is located on the flat area in the center of the photograph. Several sites near Paquimé seem to have played special roles in the political, social, and ritual lives of Paquimé and its neighbors. (Photo courtesy of Todd Pitezel.)

is a true outlier—a primate center, in the archaeological vernacular.

The mere existence of a large central community has implications about the ways in which Paquimé related to its neighbors. Comparatively, such centers are often the locations of regional economic, ritual, and political structures. They are often where elite individuals reside, so that a large proportion of decision makers and managers are concentrated in one spot. Primate centers are the points of convergence and control of regional economies, and they tend to dominate long-distance trade. To support the expenses associated with these activities, the settlements that surround the primate center often show substantial investment in facilities for the intensification of agricultural production. Finally, primate centers often serve as paramount sacred places and contain the most, largest, or most elaborate ritual architecture in their regions. Paquimé exhibits all of these characteristics along with by far the largest quantity of imported and exotic materials and the most intricate domestic spaces. These qualities include platform mounds and ball courts, both of which are common types of ceremonial architecture in Mesoamerica but are almost unknown in the Pueblo world of the U.S. Southwest to the north.

Surveys conducted in the 1990s enabled archaeologists to map the distribution of features on the landscape around Paquimé, and some interesting spatial patterns emerged from these studies.

Surveys documented an Inner Core of settlements within the radius of daily interaction, or about 15 km (9 mi), which Paquimé appears to have directly dominated. Within this Inner Core, with one notable exception, there appears to be an absence of integrative features like ball courts and platform mounds. In other words, occupants of the Inner Core apparently traveled to Paquimé to participate in major feasts, ceremonies, and other integrative

Figure 5.8. Stone-walled room block at El Pueblito. This construction, atypical for the Medio Period, underscores the special nature of this community, as does its unusual location on a high mesa away from good farming. (Photo courtesy of Todd Pitezel.)

events. The one exception is the unusual site of El Pueblito at Cerro de Moctezuma, a hilltop settlement within sight of Casas Grandes that has a very large earthen oven and a series of agricultural terraces. In addition to participating in integrative feasts and ceremonies, people of the Inner Core may have worked the agricultural terraces found on the slopes of Cerro de Moctezuma, perhaps to provide agricultural products for the elites and their ceremonies at the primate center.

Moving beyond the limit of daily interaction, from the Inner to what we call the Outer Core, located 16–30 km (9–18 mi) from the primate center, Medio Period settlements exhibit close ties to Casas Grandes. They have similar architecture and virtually identical artifact assemblages, but they also have scaled-down versions of Paquimé's integrative architecture. They may also have had somewhat more autonomy than populations in the Inner Core. Integrative features include ball courts, birdcages, and large ovens found at a range of small to very large Medio settlements in the Outer Core. This is an area where an organizational structure involving the ball game ritual and exotic goods is clearly present at a number of communities but without the pattern of monopoly seen in the immediate vicinity of Casas Grandes. Nevertheless, the Outer Core seems to have been closely tied to the primate center.

At Site 242, a small Medio Period habitation, Outer Core settlement suggests how these ties might have been maintained. Excavations at Site 242 revealed Casas Grandes–style architecture, which is recognizable by the presence of very thick adobe walls and unusually large and intricately shaped rooms. Beside the room block mound is the largest and most elaborate ball court known in the region outside of the primate center itself. Also associated with the site is a small platform mound, the only one known outside of Paquimé, and a very large system of agricultural terraces. Despite these massive facilities, however, the resident population of Site 242 was probably never more than a few dozen people. Accordingly, we see Site 242 as a focal point for the scattered rural population in this part of the Outer Core.

We suspect that the residents of Site 242 emphasized their close relation to Casas Grandes through their emulation of the domestic and ritual architecture of Casas Grandes. And the residents of Site 242 likely acted as managers who organized the scattered rural population in their vicinity. Emulation of the architecture of the primate center would have probably enhanced their local status and helped validate their legitimacy. Residents of the dispersed communities probably worked the vast terrace system beside the site to produce food for feasts at Site 242 and perhaps the primate center itself. The excess agricultural production probably qualified as "ritual labor," since it seems to have been conducted in the context of an elaborate ball court and associated platform mound.

Beyond the Outer Core, in what archaeologists call the Middle Zone, ca. 30–80 km (18–50 mi) away, communities are clearly related to Paquimé via similarities in ceramics and architecture, but sites in the Middle Zone are more widely dispersed, and there is nearly a complete absence of ball courts, platform mounds, and other integrative features.

More distant areas—including the middle Santa María valley to the southeast, the Animas area to the northwest, adjacent parts of the Sierra Madre to the west, and parts of southern Chihuahua to the south—contain extensive settlement hierarchies, as well as Casas Grandes–style ceramic assemblages and architecture. Relations between these areas and Paquimé were likely sporadic, and there is little evidence of central control of these peripheral areas.

Depending on where and by what criteria one draws boundaries, the Casas Grandes interaction sphere covered about 70,000–100,000 km² (27,000–39,000 sq mi) in northwestern Chihuahua. This is about the same size as the interacting areas of the Chaco and Hohokam of the southwestern United States. By calling these regions "interaction spheres," we are implying the existence of social, economic, and ceremonial similarities and relations among the area's communities. There is little indication of the far-flung dominance originally assumed by Di Peso, who held that Casas Grandes exercised hegemony over its near and distant neighbors. Instead, we envision a smaller, looser kind of regional structure in which the direct influence of Casas Grandes was largely confined to a relatively small area of northwestern Chihuahua.

The fall of Casas Grandes seems to have come sometime in the mid- to late 1400s, and this event has long been characterized as an abandonment of the entire region by sedentary farmers. We now question this interpretation. Fragmentation and dispersal of Paquimé's population in the late 1400s, instead of regional abandonment, is an alternative that has gained some support in recent years. Recent surveys in northwestern Chihuahua have documented a large number of very small sites with very simple ceramic assemblages. Could these sites represent the dispersed remnants of Paquimé, who broke up into small family groups after the fall of the primate center? Reading the puzzle of Casas Grandes–area settlement patterns continues to be a challenge to archaeologists, and clearly, we have more work to do.

6

CASAS GRANDES AND ITS MORE DISTANT NEIGHBORS

JOHN E. DOUGLAS AND A. C. MACWILLIAMS

The Casas Grandes region is a kaleidoscope of environmental contrasts, from the pine forests of the Sierra Madre, to the green alluvial valleys of the Sierra Madre foothills, to the vast expanses of grasslands and sand dunes undulating for hundreds of square kilometers to the east. And yet, despite the environmental diversity and vast distances, prehispanic settlements throughout northwestern Chihuahua display striking similarities in architecture, artifacts, food remains, and burial customs. Here we briefly discuss how these linkages may have been created and maintained over many centuries.

How do archaeologists identify the cultural identity of individuals in the prehispanic past and determine how people interacted in deep history? In general, we look at where and when people lived; the locations, sizes, and architectural styles of their settlements; the material attributes that they shared; and the spaces they used for public

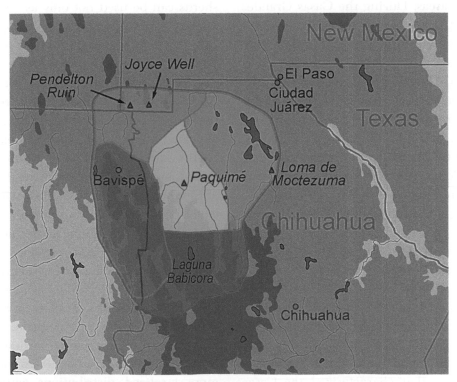

Figure 6.1. Map of farther neighbors of Paquimé. The extent and power of Paquimé's influence in more distant regions have been widely debated. (Map courtesy of A. C. MacWilliams.)

Figure 6.2. Casa Chica, a small site east of the Río Casas Grandes. This site and its ceramic types are much like sites in the El Paso area. (Photo courtesy of A. C. MacWilliams.)

gatherings. Similarities in architecture provide a good example of how people shared information over large areas. During the Casas Grandes Medio Period (A.D. 1150/1200–1450/1475), there were striking architectural similarities in houses across northwestern Chihuahua in details such as room block and plaza design, T-shaped doorway designs, and hearths with "collars" made of adobe. These characteristics appear at sites separated by almost 320 km (200 mi), a considerable distance in a pedestrian world. Crop assemblages and basic farming techniques were also shared over a large area, as were ground stone tools for milling maize and for making stone and shell jewelry and much more.

Wide sharing of styles, shapes, and decoration of pottery vessels is another material marker of Casas Grandes identity. Fired ceramics are breakable, but when pots break they fracture into sherds that are as hard as rocks and virtually indestructible. The first archaeologists to work in northwestern Chihuahua quickly recognized the kinds of pottery vessels that characterized the Casas Grandes region from the many sherds scattered over the surface of most sites. Because the dominant ceramic styles changed through time, pottery sherds can be used not only as ethnic identifiers but also as time markers. For example, during the early Viejo Period, before about A.D. 800, most pottery consisted of a plain brownware that lacked painted or textured surface treatment. Between A.D. 800 and 1200, pottery with red paint or textured designs (sometimes both on a single vessel) appeared throughout a large area centered on northwestern Chihuahua. The onset of the Medio Period around A.D. 1200 brought eye-catching polychrome ceramics to northwestern Chihuahua, which potters produced in large numbers until the abandonment of Paquimé in the mid- to late 1400s. During the Joint Casas Grandes Expedition, it soon became evident that one Medio Period type, called Babícora Polychrome, with straightforward red and black painted designs on a brown vessel, was probably made over the entire Casas Grandes area. Several other types of decorated Medio pottery, which share basic design principles, had more localized distributions within the Casas Grandes region.

Figure 6.3. Cueva de la Olla is an icon rockshelter site in the mountains west of Paquimé. The large round structure was a granary next to a small room block. This site is open to the public. (Photo courtesy of Paul Minnis.)

Widespread material identity markers occurred because of human interactions on a variety of scales: intermarriage, intercommunity ceremonies, long-distance exchange of crafts and other resources, cooperative defense against common enemies, and other practices that brought widely dispersed people into intimate contact. Exchange of goods and services created economic and social links that aided the flow of information and no doubt crystallized what it meant to be part of a common culture. At the local scale, food sharing, cooperative labor, ceremonial participation, and other face-to-face interactions helped create a recognizable Casas Grandes identity. Thus, a distinctive culture emerged around A.D. 800 in the Casas Grandes region that reached its apogee during the Medio Period and then fragmented and dispersed following the abandonment of Paquimé.

The nature of this distinct Casas Grandes culture has long intrigued archaeologists. When Europeans first entered Chihuahua in the 1500s,

they described a number of different language groups that shared many cultural practices, so a shared culture does not require that everyone speak the same language. The Pueblo people of New Mexico and Arizona share many cultural practices but speak six mutually unintelligible languages from four different language families. It is certainly possible that participants in the Casas Grandes culture were similarly diverse. In fact, we consider it unlikely that people who participated in Casas Grandes constituted one language, one ethnic group, or even one political organization. Medio Period Paquimé was probably at the apex of a multisettlement polity that connected a range of communities throughout the Inner Core, but it is unlikely, we think, that the elites of Paquimé controlled all of northwestern Chihuahua. Smaller versions of Paquimé existed beyond the Inner Core, and these populations were likely politically and ritually autonomous. Distance undoubtedly played a role in isolating some communities and creating local variations of Casas Grandes culture. Significant geographical barriers, such as mountain ranges and major drainages, almost certainly contributed as well to creating local cultural variants. Finally, local histories and local leadership assuredly shaped the distinctiveness of areas within the Casas Grandes region.

Below, we take a look at some of the regional variety in the Casas Grandes region and focus on the Viejo and Medio Periods. We do not discuss the shadowy Plainware Period, since we have so little data to go on. Further, because the abandonment of Paquimé in the fifteenth century breaks the unity of the region, we do not consider the changes that occurred after the end of the Medio Period (see discussion in the next chapter by Phillips and Gamboa). While diversity is a theme we focus on below, the Casas Grandes culture was probably a way of life that was recognizable to the people who participated in it. We suspect, though, that these ancient people, like humans everywhere, would have been more concerned in daily life with the differences between themselves and their neighbors rather than the similarities. The previous chapter looked at Paquimé and its immediate neighbors. Here we consider cultural expressions to the east, south, west, and north of Paquimé.

THE EAST

To the east of Paquimé is an arid expanse of dunes where subsistence farming would have been very difficult, and, consequently, population densities were probably always low. Salt from dry lakebeds and land routes for getting turquoise from New Mexico to the Casas Grandes valley were likely the major attractions of the region for the primate center at Paquimé. Settlements in the eastern sector probably had comparatively simple organizations in which governance focused on local issues. Perhaps more than any outlying region, however, Paquimé may have sought formal relations with groups to the east in order to ensure access to salt and to keep a critical trade route open.

THE SOUTH

The region south of Paquimé received more direct rainfall and had abundant arable land. Perhaps because of the dry farming potential of the southern region, there was apparently no need for large-scale water management systems, and human settlements remained at a fairly small scale. During the Viejo Period, people clustered in small pithouse communities thinly distributed over the landscape. Throughout the Viejo Period, day-to-day governance would likely have been at the local community level. To a modest extent, this may have changed as the Medio Period unfolded in the south. Both architecture and pottery suggest the emergence of shared religious beliefs and practices during the Medio. Compared with Paquimé, however, pottery in the south was simpler in both manufacturing technique and symbolic content, and architecture and material culture never reached the complexity of the primate center to the north.

THE WEST

In the mountains west of Paquimé and extending into northeastern Sonora, farming populations were present during both the Viejo and Medio Periods, and links to the primate center are apparent in architecture (including ball courts), pottery, and other material culture. Agricultural terraces and check dams point to organized efforts that may have required labor from multiple households, but the larger systems, some of which may indicate multisettlement polities, are found only in the largest mountain valleys and basins. There is a distinctive tenor to mountain settlements, which is evident in the use of caves for pueblo habitations and in the relative abundance of certain Casas Grandes ceramic types, such as Carretas Polychrome, a bold version of the standard Medio Period Casas Grandes polychrome pattern.

THE NORTH

Viejo Period sites have never been found along the northern edge of the Casas Grandes area, but Medio Period sites are present, suggesting that

Figure 6.4. Cuarenta Casas, one of many cliff dwellings in the Sierra Madre. This site is also open to the public. (Photo courtesy of Paul Minnis.)

Figure 6.5. A typical eastern Sonoran site with walls outlined by upright stone alignments and with a heavy scatter of artifacts. (Photo courtesy of John Douglas.)

population may have expanded into the northern reaches of northwestern Chihuahua and the U.S. Southwest during the late prehispanic period. Despite the presence of Casas Grandes–related settlements for a relatively short, 200–300-year period, evidence of a Casas Grandes "influence" in the north is nevertheless clear and relatively well studied. The Animas phase, a U.S. Southwest borderland expression coinciding with the Medio Period, includes sizeable sites and site clusters that incorporate Casas Grandes ceramics and architectural features. Ball courts, collared hearths, and a variety of Casas Grandes pottery styles, including the signature style from the central area, Ramos Polychrome, are all present in the area. Archaeologists have cited migration, trade relations, and shared ideology as likely explanations for these northernmost Casas Grandes expressions.

THE SHARED AND THE UNIQUE

Membership in Casas Grandes culture ultimately had its roots in many generations of relations and shared ideology and material culture. Commonly held pottery and architecture, two of the most persistent material expressions from the past, are likely indicative of a deeper mingling of values, ideologies, and lifeways, even though these nonmaterial aspects of culture are always difficult to comprehend through material evidence alone. This is one reason why the kind of regional comparative analysis presented here is so important. From this perspective, the specific religious practices the VanPools discussed in a previous chapter probably evolved from local innovations fueled by specialization, a large face-to-face population, and ideas about the sacred that spread throughout Mesoamerica and its northern frontier during the late prehispanic period. Undoubtedly, some of the religious beliefs and practices also had ancient local roots stretching back to Viejo times and beyond. And given Paquimé's large public ritual setting, it is likely that people traveled from considerable distances to observe the spectacular rituals of the primate center and take back to their distant homes stories and objects relating to the grandeur of Paquimé. By doing so, pilgrims would have influenced others in their homeland to make the journey, and local leaders might have emulated Paquiméan practices to enhance their own power and authority.

Comparative studies generally do not support the notion that Casas Grandes was a hegemonic regional polity. But did Casas Grandes influence and create a strong ritual flavor? Yes. Did it control? Probably not. Paquimé was no doubt the center of regional interaction. And it maintained regional connections through the long-distance trade of goods, both practical, such as salt, and value laden, such as turquoise and shell. The society that developed in the valley of the Casas Grandes River had obvious attractions for isolated mountain cliff dwellers, dryland farmers to the south, and communities that sprang up to the north and east that were involved in the long-distance exchange of goods, from bison products to turquoise. Naturally, archaeologists would like to know more about how Casas Grandes society worked and how its leadership organized it into communities and polities across the region. Needless to say, we need more studies, especially more refined comparative research of the history and workings of northwestern Chihuahua's social, economic, and political life.

7

THE END OF PAQUIMÉ AND THE CASAS GRANDES CULTURE

DAVID A. PHILLIPS, JR., AND EDUARDO GAMBOA CARRERA

In 1536 Spanish explorer Álvar Núñez Cabeza de Vaca passed through the southern end of the Casas Grandes area but failed to report inhabited villages. Three decades later, the Ibarra expedition was more specific. As the Spaniards entered Chihuahua, they discovered "abandoned houses of two and three stories." When the expedition reached Paquimé, it too lay empty. By the mid-1500s, it seems, the Casas Grandes culture had collapsed. But how much earlier did this happen?

WHEN WAS PAQUIMÉ ABANDONED?

The latest surviving tree ring from Paquimé dates to A.D. 1338—two centuries before Cabeza de

Figure 7.1. The early Spanish church at the Convento Site with JCGE's excavation crew members. The end of Paquimé and the indigenous occupation during the early Spanish occupation remains a major research topic. Unlike many locations in the SW/NW, there is no obvious continuity between archaeological groups and modern indigenous communities.

Vaca's travels through western Chihuahua—but this date is misleading. Thanks to compulsive wood trimming followed by rotting, multiple tree rings are missing, especially the critical outside rings, from every timber recovered from Paquimé. Based on Jeffrey Dean and John Ravesloot's computer simulations, we believe that construction at Paquimé continued into the 1440s. Combining this result with information from radiocarbon dating, pottery analysis, and obsidian hydration studies, we believe the occupation at Paquimé probably ended about 1450 or perhaps a little later.

WHEN DID THE CULTURE END?

As Di Peso pointed out, the Casas Grandes culture could have outlived its principal center. We therefore reviewed the information from other Casas Grandes sites and found a rapid fall-off in radiocarbon dates about 1450. It seems that the entire culture ended when Paquimé did. This statement may be too categorical, however. It ignores the possibility that a few communities lingered, perhaps for generations, after the collapse of Paquimé itself. We know of three Casas Grandes sites with post-1450 radiocarbon dates: Casa de Robles, in the Sierra Madre; Ojo de Agua, in Sonora; and Villa Ahumada, in the desert lowlands of eastern Chihuahua. At this point, unfortunately, it is unclear whether the late dates are evidence of relict Casas Grandes populations or "noise" introduced by the dating process itself.

Casas Grandes pottery is sometimes found outside its area of origin as a trade item. Many of the sites where it wound up are dated and based on the assumption that Casas Grandes pottery ceased to be an important trade ware after 1450. The simplest explanation is that, by then, the pottery was no longer being made. In summary, the available evidence, though far from complete, suggests that the abandonment of Paquimé in about 1450 coincided with a general collapse in the Casas Grandes culture. However, we have yet to work out the details of regional depopulation— whether it happened quickly, as a single wave of emigration, or slowly and in dribbles.

WHAT HAPPENED?

If we accept for the moment that we know when the Casas Grandes culture collapsed, we also need to ask how it happened. We have one native account: the Casas people moved north after a conflict with people to the west. So perhaps the Casas people fought with Sonoran peoples (the Opata?), after which they retreated north to join today's Puebloans.

Archaeologists have suggested a different outcome: the Casas Grandes people became the Opata. That tribe formed a linguistic "wedge" in the historical distribution of Piman speakers, and one way to derive the Opata wedge is to have the Casas Grandes people leave northwestern Chihuahua in favor of northeastern Sonora, pushing resident Piman speakers to the side.

WHY?

Di Peso tied the fall of Paquimé to turmoil in Mesoamerica, but as we now understand, the timing of events makes that scenario unlikely. At the moment, there is no consensus about the actual reason for the abandonment of that site. We therefore present, briefly, a model developed by Eduardo Gamboa that describes the collapse of the Paquimé-centered social system. As the Casas Grandes elite took form, it turned to southern Mexico for models of ritual and social behavior and then imposed those new ways on its own society. In doing so, the elite created a contrast between traditional society (most people) and its own foreign-inspired practices. The resulting social tensions could have boiled over, resulting in internal violence and cultural collapse. In other words, the end may not have been due to an external cause such as drought or attack.

If this "internal conflict" model seems extreme, consider Awatovi in the Hopi country, which sparked its own destruction by other Hopi villages through its renewed acceptance of a foreign (Spanish) religion. If Paquimé's elite imposed exotic religious and social ideas on the rest of the populace, might the town similarly have invited its destruction by outraged inhabitants of the surrounding villages?

THE WAY FORWARD

Recently, Michael Whalen and Paul Minnis proposed that the collapse of Paquimé was linked to sudden changes in the culture's elaborate polychrome pottery, not to a sudden departure of the local population. If Whalen and Minnis are correct, why haven't we seen strong evidence of late, post-Paquimé archaeological sites? Because we haven't looked! In the past, archaeologists tended to investigate sites with elaborately painted pottery. If future work seeks out sites where the pottery is simpler, we may find that, just as Di Peso once proposed, the Casas Grandes people outlasted Paquimé. In that case, we don't need to think in terms of a regional catastrophe that drove everyone away. Instead, we could look for a less extreme source of change, one that led part of the culture to collapse while allowing part of it to survive. It is an intriguing thought that we hope will turn into answers as fieldwork continues.

Looking far beyond the Casas Grandes River valley to the rest of the SW/NW, we should also consider another explanation. The abandonment of Casas Grandes around 1450 coincides with the collapse and dispersal of Classic Hohokam populations in the Gila and Salt River valleys of southern Arizona, the depopulation of the Mogollon highlands and adjacent areas in western New Mexico and eastern Arizona, and the abandonment of Ancestral Puebloan sites in the upper and middle Little Colorado River valley of northeastern Arizona. Mid- to late fifteenth-century population disruptions in the SW/NW were so severe that when Coronado and his army marched through northern Sonora to the Zuni River valley in the spring and summer of 1540, they described the 645 k (400 mi) they traversed as *la tierra despoblado* (the land without people). Because dating abandonments is an imprecise science—as opposed to tree-ring dating of when a house was built—we can't be sure that these loosely correlated abandonment events were actually contemporaneous.

As usual, more research is needed. At this point, it is enough to suggest that the abandonment of Paquimé was not an isolated event.

8

PAQUIMÉ

A REVISION OF ITS RELATIONS TO THE SOUTH AND WEST

JOSÉ LUIS PUNZO DÍAZ AND M. ELISA VILLALPANDO CANCHOLA

In 1980, when coming back to Sonora from the Mogollon Conference at Las Cruces, New Mexico, Charles Di Peso invited Beatriz Braniff, Ana María Álvarez, and Elisa Villalpando to spend a night at the Amerind Foundation to talk with him about recent discoveries at Huatabampo in southern Sonora. They followed dinner with very late conversation and Italian wine. He was truly enthusiastic about the new discoveries in Sonora and northern Sinaloa, where Álvarez and Villalpando, then young archaeologists, were conducting research. We can only imagine how excited he would be

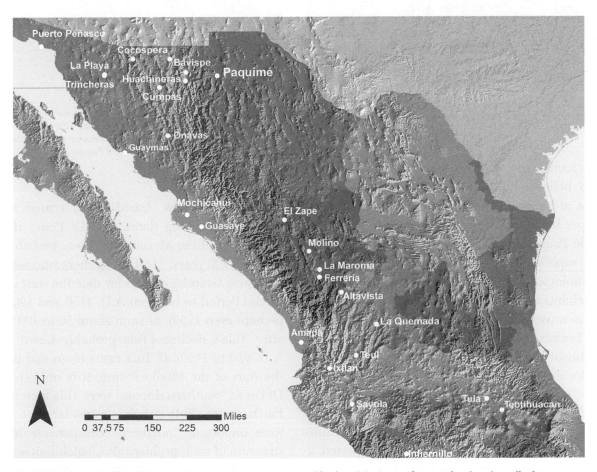

Figure 8.1. Map of northern Mexico with major archaeological sites. Northern Mexico is a large and archaeologically diverse region and not just a hinterland between the U.S. Southwest and Mesoamerica. (Map courtesy of José Luis Punzo.)

today after so much research has been conducted in and around Paquimé and throughout northern and central Mexico.

As late as the mid-1970s, the dominant interpretation of Paquimé was summarized in the subtitle of Di Peso's eight-volume masterpiece: *A Fallen Trading Center of the Gran Chichimeca*. Di Peso was convinced that a sophisticated group of merchants, known as pochteca, from Mesoamerica arrived in the Casas Grandes River valley and inspired the local "Chichimeca" population to build the city of Paquimé. But who were these

worship of several Mesoamerican gods, including Tezcatlipoca (the Smoking Mirror), Quetzalcóatl (the Feather Serpent), and Huitzilopochtli (the Left Hummingbird). Di Peso drew specific linkages between Paquimé and Tula in central Mexico. Di Peso believed that Toltec elements diffused into the northern Mesoamerican frontier via the Pacific coast and the Chalchihuites culture of Zacatecas and Durango, finally arriving at Paquimé during the eleventh century to initiate the various changes that characterized the Medio Period.

Figure 8.2. A representation of a Mesoamerican pochteca, or long-distance trader, who Di Peso argued were important to the rise of Paquimé.

Figure 8.3. The famous warrior figures atop a pyramid at Tula. Di Peso originally thought that pochtecas from Tula organized Paquimé into a major trading center. Subsequent research has shown that Tula ended before the rise of Paquimé. (Photo courtesy of Susan Bridgemon.)

merchants, and where did they come from? Di Peso believed that they came from the Pacific coast of Mexico, bringing with them not only the copper bells, marine shell, and parrots that have made Paquimé justifiably famous but also things like sophisticated hydraulic systems and other technological advancements. Presumably, these merchants arrived in the Casas Grandes River valley as waves of immigrants or through conquest, and because of their knowledge and abilities, they established themselves as co-leaders who taught the local population.

Di Peso believed that the change between the Viejo and Medio Periods was rapid and dramatic, sparked by the arrival of merchant immigrants. The merchants not only transported a variety of exotic products from the west coast but also brought religious cults focused on the

We know now, based on a reanalysis of Paquimé's tree-ring dates, that Di Peso's dating of the start of the Medio Period was probably off by some 200 years. Most researchers who work in the Casas Grandes area today date the start of the Medio Period to between A.D. 1150 and 1200 (or perhaps even 1250), or from about 50 to 100 years after Tula's decline (Tula probably lasted from A.D. 950 to 1150). If Tula came to an end before the start of the Medio Period, it is unlikely that Di Peso's "southern donors" were Tula merchants. Furthermore, Tula scholars consider that there were important "northern" components in the structure of such prehispanic Chalchihuites cities as La Quemada and Altavista in Zacatecas and Durango. Some scholars consider the presence of

Figure 8.4. La Quemada, an important Mesoamerican center in Zacatecas. (Photo courtesy of José Luis Punzo.)

Figure 8.5. Altavista, a major Mesoamerican center located on the border between Zacatecas and Durango. (Photo courtesy of José Luis Punzo.)

Figure 8.6. (left) Decorated *Glycymeris* bracelets from Cerro de Trincheras, Sonora. Shell was a common trade item, and most shell came from the Gulf of California in Mexico. (Photo courtesy of Elisa Villalpando.)

tzompantli (trophy skulls), feathered snakes, *chacmool*s (ritual tables for sacrifice), and other items as indicators of a strong relation between Tula and the Chalchihuites culture (other scholars see northern groups contributing some of these traits to Tula). Chalchihuites culture was present from A.D. 200 to 1350 on the eastern flank of the Sierra Madre Occidental in the states of Zacatecas and Durango in Mexico.

When Di Peso conducted his pioneering work in northwestern Chihuahua, archaeologists knew very little about the Chalchihuites culture of north-central Mexico. Recent work in Zacatecas and Durango and along the coast in Sinaloa and Nayarit has improved local chronologies, so we now know that the Chalchihuites occupation of Durango and Amapa in Nayarit dates well before the start of the Paquimé Medio Period. Therefore, they were a more likely source for the various southern traits found at Paquimé. For example, Di Peso interpreted a red ceramic drum and many drum fragments from Paquimé to be an important indicator of Mesoamerican relationships—a direct connection between Paquimé and the west coast of Mexico. More recent research has documented similar drums in many sites in western Mexico and even in Cañón del Molino, an important Chalchihuites culture site, in the Guatimape valley, Durango. Di Peso also argued that the pseudocloisonné technique found at Paquimé could only

have come from direct contact with Tula and western Mexico, but we now have multiple examples from Michoacán to Sinaloa and inland as far as Durango.

In summary, the new data and dates gathered since the Joint Casas Grandes Expedition show that many foreign artifacts date well before the Medio Period. Consequently, these data do not support the interaction model of specialized merchants as the founders of Paquimé. Either these artifacts are heirlooms, or their presence at Paquimé suggests long-distance relationships with the south during Casas Grandes' Viejo Period. In order to develop a better understanding of such relations, we need a much deeper regional chronological perspective.

Di Peso based many of his trading-center arguments on imported seashells found in rather spectacular abundance at Paquimé (1.5 tons representing over 70 species of bivalves, univalves, and saphopods). Di Peso saw a significant increase in shell between the Viejo, when shell was used mostly for personal adornment, and the start of the Medio Period, when Paquimé began amassing large quantities of marine shell for trade and as socioreligious artifacts associated with various Mesoamerican religious cults. Di Peso argued that most of the marine shell found at Paquimé, especially the millions of *Nassarius* species, came from the coast near Guaymas and Sonora and beaches to the south. He also claimed that some species found at Paquimé—such as the red shell oyster, black murex (*Hexaplex nigritus*), and the shells of *Persicula bandera*—could have only come from waters south of the Tropic of Cancer (around the present-day city of Mazatlán, Sinaloa). Di Peso went on to propose a trade route to the west coast that went from Paquimé over the mountain range to Nacori Chico and from there through the Nuri Valley to the Cedros River down to the mouth of the Mátape and Yaqui Rivers.

There are at least two problems with Di Peso's proposed shell trade route. First, most of the 70 identified species of shell found at Paquimé are not limited to the Guaymas area but can be found along the entire coast of the Gulf of California. Second, no one has ever found evidence of Casas

Figure 8.7. Massive terraces at the northern end of Cerro de Trincheras. These terraces formed the foundations for houses. This site was a major regional center in northern Sonora. (Photo courtesy of Elisa Villalpando.)

Grandes material culture (ceramics, etc.) in the Mátape and Yaqui coastal areas. In short, there is little if any empirical evidence to support Di Peso's route.

Very little was known about the Trincheras Tradition in northern Sonora when Di Peso proposed that there was a Hohokam supply route from the Guaymas area to the north. Today we know that Cerro de Trincheras had no Mesoamerican connections, but it is possible that traders transported a significant amount of shell from the Gulf of California to Paquimé as finished ornaments through an east–west interaction axis that followed the interriverine valleys of the Sierra Madre

Occidental. It is also possible, we think, that Paquiméans traded marine shell for polychrome ceramics as part of a trans–Sierra Madre prestige economy.

Another key element in Di Peso's trading center model was commerce in turquoise that he argued came from New Mexico mines. Unfortunately, even though turquoise was an important commodity during the Postclassic Period in central Mexico, the provenience of most of the turquoise remains very much in doubt. Green and blue stones, sometimes called "cultural turquoise," were available from many locations closer to central Mexico, and these might have helped satisfy the demand for green and blue stones. An example is a cluster of mines in the northern end of the Chalchihuites area, where amazonite substituted for the scarcity of real turquoise.

The best-known example of Paquimé's interaction with the south is the presence of exotic birds, most of them identified as the scarlet or "red" macaw (*Ara macao*). Nevertheless, early Spanish explorers noted that the breeding of birds was a generalized practice in many places of northern Mexico. Di Peso presents evidence of bird breeders in the Huasteca in northeastern Mexico, but there was also some bird breeding among the Acaxées, who lived along the border of Durango, Sinaloa, and Chihuahua in the Sierra Madre Occidental. These groups traveled during colonial times with red and green macaws and parrots from the highlands as part of their more precious possessions. In addition, the historic depth of this practice could go back farther in time in this region, as three fragments of stone rings, similar to the ones identified as macaws' nest doors in Paquimé, were found in the Chalchihuites site of La Ferrería, Durango, where they could date as early as A.D. 600–1000.

Figure 8.8. A Villa Ahumada (a Casas Grandes style) vessel from Cerro de Trincheras. (Photo courtesy of Elisa Villalpando.)

Another element that Di Peso noted as evidence of Paquimé's relationship to parts of Mesoamerica is the presence of trophy skulls, a practice apparently dating to the beginning of the Medio Period in the Casas Grandes region. Di Peso correlates the presence of tzompantli at Paquimé with those found at Tula, Tenochtitlan, and the Maya area. However, although it was not generally known at the time Di Peso worked in Chihuahua, this practice was also common among the Chalchihuites people in Durango, Zacatecas,

and northern Jalisco since the beginning of the first millennium. In other words, the practice at Paquimé might have had a much closer source than central Mexico.

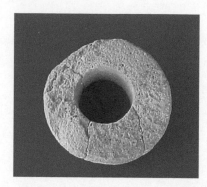

Figure 8.9. A possible parrot cage stone from La Ferrería, Durango, Mexico. This may indicate widespread macaw raising in northern Mexico. (Courtesy of José Luis Punzo.)

Metal artifacts and metallurgy were also noted as evidence of direct relationships between central Mesoamerica and Paquimé. Although Di Peso reports some copper artifacts unique to Paquimé, he suggested that most of the copper artifacts produced by artists during the Medio Period at Paquimé were similar to Mesoamerican forms, providing a direct link to the high cultures of the Mesoamerican interior. Unfortunately, no firm evidence of copper smelting has ever been recovered from Paquimé, which raises serious doubts about the role of metallurgy in the Paquimé craft industry. Most if not all copper artifacts found at Paquimé were probably imported from western Mexico, probably via Chalchihuites or Aztlan intermediaries.

Figure 8.10. Copper bells from cremations at Cerro de Trincheras, Sonora. Copper was fabricated in western Mexico and was traded widely in the SW/NW. (Photo courtesy of Elisa Villalpando.)

In sum, data collected in recent years in intermediate regions of Mesoamerica's northwestern frontier allow us to refine our understanding of the relationships between Paquimé and Mesoamerica, especially with the groups who lived along the Pacific coast and inland in the Chalchihuites area of Durango and Zacatecas. There is still much to do. Different models should be explored about the complex interactions between Paquimé and its various prehispanic neighbors to the south. In the meantime, we think it is likely that there were complex interactions between northwestern Chihuahua and regions to the south beginning much earlier than the Casas Grandes Medio Period. These interactions are reflected in archaeological materials recovered from both Chihuahua and regions to the south. Although foreign objects indicate the existence of extensive trade, the data do not support the idea of Mesoamerican mercantilism and exploitation as an explanation of prehispanic developments at Paquimé. It seems more likely to us that the acquisition of nonlocal goods reflects a prestige goods economy, which results from the intensification of social relations among elites from two or more ranked societies. In other words, the presence of prestige goods was probably a consequence rather than a cause of social differentiation and the emergence of ranked societies in northern Mexico. Northern Mexico was a dynamic cultural region during the prehispanic times where ranked societies established long-distance relations with other ranked societies. The exchange of rare or exotic objects helped create and validate social ranking in diverse environments and over extended time periods.

Figure 8.11. Pyramid 1 at La Ferrería, an important site near Durango City. (Photo courtesy of José Luis Punzo.)

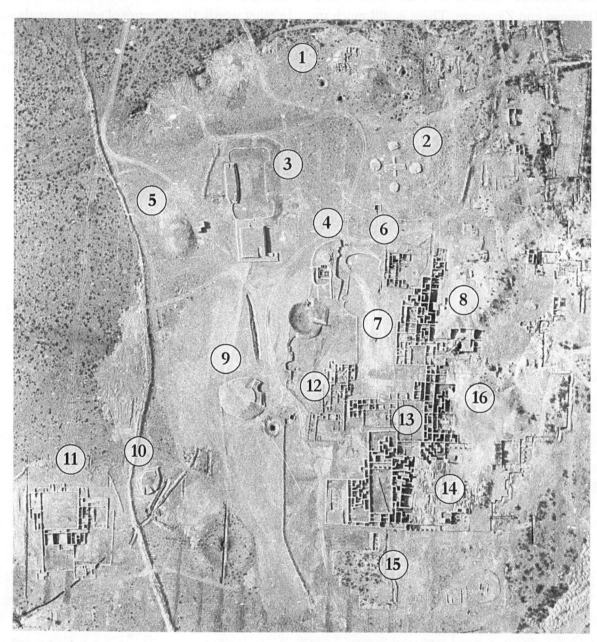

Major excavation units of the Joint Casas Grandes Expedition. (Photo courtesy of the Amerind Foundation.)*

*   The site descriptions and map in this appendix originally appeared in *Ancient Paquimé and the Casas Grandes World*, edited by Paul E. Minnis and Michael E. Whalen (Tucson: University of Arizona Press, 2015).

APPENDIX
PAQUIMÉ SITE MAP AND DESCRIPTIONS

A SHORT DESCRIPTION OF PAQUIMÉ

Paquimé is a remarkable community, much of which was revealed by JCGE's research. Below are very brief descriptions of JCGE's major excavation units.

UNIT 1: MOUND OF THE PIT OVENS. Located at the north end of the site, this unit consists of 2 room blocks with about 10 rooms and 4 exceptionally large earthen ovens surround a mound composed in part of cooking debris from the ovens.

UNIT 2: MOUND OF THE CROSS. A low cross-shaped feature slightly less than 40 m in length with a low circular mound at the end of each cross arm. This feature may mark specific sunrises.

UNIT 3: BALL COURT I. This is the largest ball court at Paquimé and probably in the Casas Grandes region. Its flat field is about 19 × 50 m and is flanked on one side by a low rectangular mound and a taller square mound on its southern end.

UNIT 4: MOUND OF THE OFFERINGS. This eccentrically shaped mound is at the northwestern corner of the main plaza near a reservoir. Embedded within the main mound features are three small tombs. One held a finely made ground stone altar, and the other two contained very special secondary burials. An unusual set of adobe-walled enclosures are present in an enclosed plaza within the southern portion of this unit.

UNIT 5: MOUND 1-5. This is a mound south of Ball Court I. It was most likely an incomplete ceremonial mound, a stockpile of construction material, or a trash deposit.

UNIT 6: HOUSE-CLUSTER. This is a one- and two-story adobe-walled room block with approximately 30 rooms of different periods surrounding an enclosed plaza. Viejo Period pithouses were present.

UNIT 7: RETAINING WALL AND ROOM. The western edge of the main plaza is demarcated by a low stone wall with a small embedded room having a *jacal* front wall facing the plaza.

UNIT 8: HOUSE OF THE WELL. This unit is one of the largest multistoried room blocks at Paquimé with about 75 excavated rooms and multiple enclosed plazas. It is named after the walk-in well, a water shrine below one of the plazas. In addition to the many domestic rooms, several rooms contained vast quantities of goods, such as shell, unworked minerals, and whole vessels.

UNIT 9: MOUND OF THE HEROES. A large, roughly circular mound, 55 × 40 m, dominates this unit. It is next to what is likely the largest earthen pit oven in the SW/NW and other features interpreted by Di Peso as pithouses.

UNIT 10: MOUND OF THE BIRD. This large earthen mound, approximately 24 × 17 m, is shaped like a decapitated bird.

UNIT 11: HOUSE OF THE SERPENT. This complex is located at the far western portion of the site. It is a single-story room block with approximately 30 rooms and 4 walled plazas. Just to the west is a low mound shaped as a feathered/horned effigy about 115 m long.

UNIT 12: HOUSE OF THE MACAWS. This set of single-story high rooms is named for the plaza with the best-preserved macaw pens and with numerous macaw burials. About 35 rooms surround 3 to 5 plazas.

UNIT 13: HOUSE OF THE DEAD. This unit of 19 excavated rooms and 2 plazas yielded an unusually large number of burials. One of the plazas had a large number of turkey pens and turkey burials. One room contained a unique subfloor burial chamber interpreted as the interment of a very special person.

UNIT 14: HOUSE OF THE PILLARS. This unit is one of the large, multistoried set of room blocks with around up to 6 plazas and what is interpreted as a small ball court enclosed in one of the plazas. Several rooms in this unit have notably eccentric shapes that likely indicate use other than domestic. One of the site's most impressive colonnades faces south from this unit.

UNIT 15: HOUSE-CLUSTER. This largely unexcavated unit was estimated to have had about 30 one-story rooms and at least one plaza. Two rooms were excavated by the JCGE.

UNIT 16: HOUSE OF THE SKULLS. Named for "trophy" skulls found in a cruciform room, this unit is one of the large multistoried sets of room blocks and has at least two plazas. Thirty-nine rooms were excavated.

UNIT 17: BALL COURT II. This large ball court at the southern end of the site is much like Ball Court I but has been partially destroyed by an arroyo.

UNIT 18. This unit at the south end of the site had a small room block and a rectangular room on a platform, a unique architectural feature at Paquimé.

UNITS 19–23: HOUSE-CLUSTERS AND NORTH-HOUSE. This units are largely unexcavated room blocks.

WATER SYSTEM. The water distribution system at Paquimé is truly remarkable; nothing like it existed in the prehispanic SW/NW. A canal (5 km long) brought water from the dependable Ojo Varaleño north of the site to a reservoir that diverted water into canals snaking throughout the room blocks. The system was changed, and a new reservoir constructed. A series of drainage canals removed water from the adobe room blocks.

ACKNOWLEDGMENTS

This book was written and illustrated for a general audience as a companion volume to the more technical *Ancient Paquimé and the Casas Grandes World* (University of Arizona Press, 2015). Both books celebrate the seventy-fifth anniversary of the Amerind Foundation in 2012 and the fortieth anniversary of the publication of *Casas Grandes: A Fallen Trading Center of the Gran Chichimeca* in 1974.

The editors have many people to thank. First and foremost, our gratitude goes to the staff and sponsors of the Joint Casas Grandes Expedition, especially to the late Charles C. Di Peso and Eduardo Contreras Sánchez, who codirected the Casas Grandes excavations, and to the Amerind Foundation and the Instituto Nacional de Antropología e Historia, who collaborated to make the project possible. Special thanks also to Amerind founder William Shirley Fulton, who helped conceive the project and provided critical funds for the fieldwork, the subsequent analysis, and the write-up.

This volume comes out of an advanced seminar held at the Amerind Foundation in the fall of 2012. We thank the staff of the Amerind for its hospitality, especially Amerind director John Ware, who was the developmental editor of the book, and associate curator Ron Bridgemon, who led the book's design team. We thank Leigh McDonald, art director and book designer at the University of Arizona Press, for her work on the cover and interior designs, as well as editor-in-chief Allyson Carter, director Kathryn Conrad, and the rest of the University of Arizona Press staff. Financial support from the Arizona Archaeological and Historical Society, which made the publication of this book possible, is gratefully acknowledged.

The volume was made possible by all the researchers who have followed in the giant footsteps of Di Peso and Contreras. One of those researchers, Linda Cordell, participated in the seminar and authored a chapter in the technical volume but died suddenly before work on this volume began. All of us who knew Linda will miss her deeply, and the loss to archaeology is incalculable. It is also with great sorrow that we learned of the death of our beloved colleague, Jane H. Kelley, as this volume went to press. Jane was and will continue to be an inspiration to generations of archaeologists.

Finally, the volume editors wish to thank Julián Hernández Chávez for his help and friendship over the years, and we extend a heartfelt thank you as well to Arturo Guevara Sánchez, an inspiring and pioneering scholar of Chihuahuan archaeology.

SUGGESTED READINGS

Braniff Cornejo, Beatriz. 2001. *La Gran Chichimeca, el lugar de las rocas secas.* CONACULTA and Jaca Books, Mexico City.

Cordell, Linda S., and Maxine E. McBrinn. 2012. *Archaeology of the Southwest.* 3rd ed. Left Coast Press, Walnut Creek, California.

Di Peso, Charles C., John Rinaldo, and Gloria Fenner. 1974. *Casas Grandes: A Fallen Trading Center of the Gran Chichimeca.* Northland Press, Flagstaff, Arizona.

Lekson, Stephen H. 2008. *A History of the Ancient Southwest.* School for Advanced Research Press, Santa Fe.

McGuire, Randall H., and M. Elisa Villalpando Canchola. 2011. *Excavations at Cerro de Trincheras.* Arizona State Museum Archaeological Series. 2 vols. University of Arizona, Tucson.

Minnis, Paul E., and Michael E. Whalen. 2015. *Ancient Paquimé and the Casas Grandes World.* University of Arizona Press, Tucson.

Newell, Gillian, and Emiliano Gallaga. 2001. *Surveying the Archaeology of Northwest Mexico.* University of Utah Press, Salt Lake City.

Plog, Stephen. 2008. *Ancient People of the American Southwest.* Thames and Hudson, New York.

Punzo Diaz, José Luis, and Marie-Areti Hers. 2013. *Historia de Durango: Época antigua.* Instituto de Investigaciones Históricas, Universidad Juárez del Estado Durango, Durango.

Rakita, Gordon F. M. 2009. *Ancestors and Elites: Emergent Complexity and Ritual Practices in the Casas Grandes Polity.* AltaMira Press, Lanham, Maryland.

Riley, Carroll L. 2005. *Becoming Aztlan: Mesoamerican Influences in the Greater Southwest (AD 1200–1500).* University of Utah Press, Salt Lake City.

Schaafsma, Curtis F., and Carroll L. Riley. 1999. *The Casas Grandes World.* University of Utah Press, Salt Lake City.

VanPool, Christine S., and Todd L. VanPool. 2007. *Signs of the Casas Grandes Shamans.* University of Utah Press, Salt Lake City.

Whalen, Michael E., and Paul E. Minnis. 2001. *Casas Grandes and Its Hinterland: Prehistoric Regional Organization in Northwest Mexico.* University of Arizona Press, Tucson.

——. 2009. *The Neighbors of Casas Grandes: Excavating Medio Period Communities of Northwest Chihuahua, Mexico.* University of Arizona Press, Tucson.

Woosley, Anne I., and John C. Ravesloot. 1993. *Culture and Contact: Charles C. Di Peso's Gran Chichimeca.* University of New Mexico Press, Albuquerque.

CONTRIBUTORS

Rafael Cruz Antillón (graduate of the Escuela Nacional de Antropología e Historia) is an investigator with INAH-Chihuahua. He has conducted numerous research projects in the Casas Grandes region during the past two decades.

John E. Douglas (Ph.D., University of Arizona) is professor of anthropology at the University of Montana. He has conducted excavation and survey in the Animas region of southeastern Arizona and the Sierra region of eastern Sonora.

Eduardo Gamboa Carrera (graduate, Escuela Nacional de Antropología e Historia) is an investigator with INAH-Chihuahua. He has worked in the Casas Grandes region for many years, especially communities in the Sierra Madre.

Jane H. Kelley (Ph.D., Harvard University) was a professor emerita of archaeology at the University of Calgary. She had been involved in west-central Chihuahuan archaeology as codirector of a long-term project since 1990.

A. C. MacWilliams (Ph.D., University of Arizona) is currently an adjunct professor of archaeology with the University of Calgary. He has been involved in Chihuahuan archaeology since 1990.

Paul E. Minnis (Ph.D., University of Michigan) is a professor emeritus of anthropology at the University of Oklahoma. He has conducted research on the prehispanic ethnobotany and archaeology of the Casas Grandes region since 1984.

David A. Phillips, Jr. (Ph.D., University of Arizona), is curator of archaeology at the Maxwell Museum of Anthropology, University of New Mexico, and a research associate professor of anthropology at the university. Since the early 1990s he has participated in fieldwork in central and west-central Chihuahua.

Todd A. Pitezel (Ph.D., University of Arizona) is assistant curator of archaeology and the Arizona Antiquities Act administrator at Arizona State Museum. He has conducted archaeological research in the Casas Grandes area since 1998.

José Luis Punzo Díaz (Ph.D., Escuela Nacional de Antropología e Historia) has conducted archaeology work in northern Mexico since 1994.

Gordon F. M. Rakita (Ph.D., University of New Mexico) is professor of anthropology at the University of North Florida. His research has focused on the Casas Grandes culture area for nearly 20 years.

Michael T. Searcy (Ph.D., University of Oklahoma) is an assistant professor of anthropology at Brigham Young University. He has worked in the Casas Grandes region for a decade.

Christine S. VanPool (Ph.D., University of New Mexico) is an associate professor of anthropology at the University of Missouri. For the past eighteen years she has focused on ritual and pottery symbolism in the Casas Grandes world.

Todd L. VanPool (Ph.D., University of New Mexico) is an associate professor of anthropology at the University of Missouri. His most recent field research has focused on 76 Draw, a Medio Period Casas Grandes settlement in southern New Mexico.

M. Elisa Villalpando Canchola (graduate, Escuela Nacional de Antropología and Estudios Históricos of El Colegio de México) has been a researcher with INAH-Sonora since 1979. She has directed and participated in many archaeological projects in Sonora.

Michael E. Whalen (Ph.D., University of Michigan) is a professor in the Department of Anthropology at the University of Tulsa. He has conducted research in the Casas Grandes area since 1989.

INDEX